C000212544

BOMBERS OVER SUSSEX

Pat Burgess and Andy Saunders

Cover: (left) Houses at Albert Road, Bognor, which took a direct hit on 5th February 1943. At "Seacroft" Mildred Gooder was killed and Madeline Harrington at "Shorebank".

(right) The tail section of a Junkers 188 shot down at Hale Farm, Withyham, on 24th February 1944.

May the sacrifices made by those airmen in the service of their respective countries and the scale of civilian loss of life resulting from aerial warfare over the county not be quickly or carelessly forgotten. This book is a tribute to all who suffered.

ANDY SAUNDERS & PAT BURGESS

First published April 1995

ISBN 1 873793 51 0

Design Deborah Goodridge

Published by Middleton Press
Easebourne Lane
Midhurst
West Sussex
GU29 9AZ
Tel: (01730) 813169

Printed & bound by Biddles Ltd,
Guildford and Kings Lynn

CONTENTS

Map of the administrative boundaries effective in 1940 and used throughout this book. The figures are the page numbers, listed above.

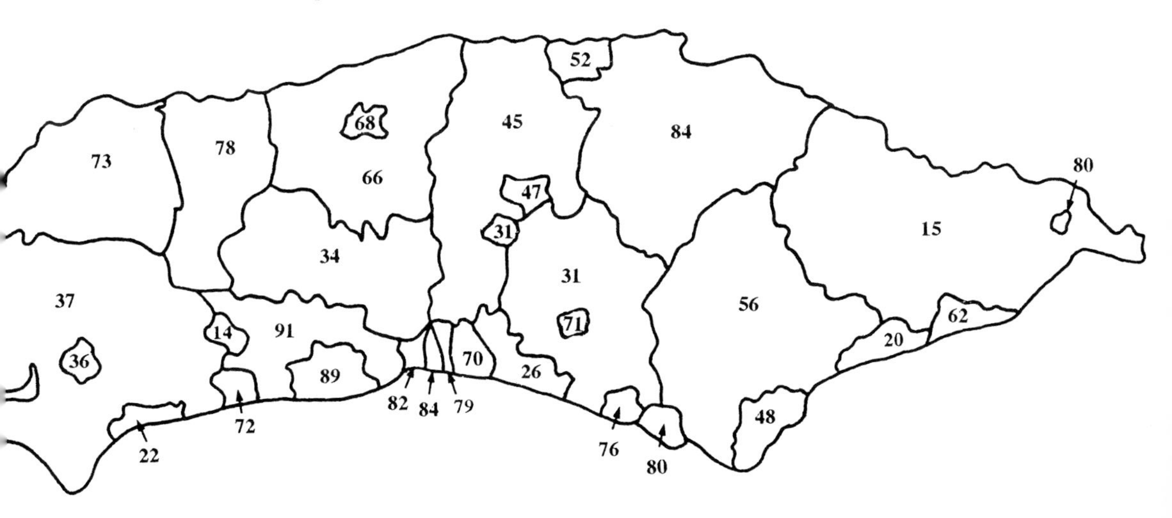

ACKNOWLEDGEMENTS

Many good friends and fellow-enthusiasts have gone to great lengths to help us during the preparation of this book. In particular our thanks go to; Peter Foote, Nancy Woodall, Bryon Purdey,Alan Readman, Roger Freeman, Steve Hall, George Morgan, Ron Gammage, Chris Thomas, Gordon Anckorn, "Freddie" Moureau, Flt. Lt. Chris Goss, Eileen Saunders, Freda Mitchell, Terry Connolly, Cliff White, Bob Elliston, Dennis Cullum, Reg Randell, Winston and Gordon Ramsey, Ian Hutton, Wg. Cdr. Keith Hopkins, Roy Hathaway, Bob Benton, Stan Bishop, Pat Batty and Alf Cave.

A special thank you goes to Brian Bridges who has offered friendly help over many years in our quest for information.

Also, special mention must be made of Mrs. Jenny Hickman who once again allowed us to use pictures from the wonderful photographs in the collection of her late father, Mr. Frank Lalouette. What a pity that collections like this do not exist for towns in Sussex other than Bognor Regis!

As always, help has been freely given by the Records Offices of East and West Sussex, the various county libraries, Imperial War Museum, RAF Museum, Public Record Office, Commonwealth War Graves Commission, German War Graves Service, American Battle Monuments Commission and the Bundesarchiv in Germany. Over the years much help has also been given us by the Air Historical Branch of the MOD, particularly by Richard King.

Vic Mitchell of Middleton Press has continued to lend his support and encouragement to the project and his daughter, Deborah Goodridge, has done a splendid job of putting the various packages together into three volumes. However, before we even got to the production stage Trevor and Stella Linford have done a magnificent job producing the manuscript - ably assisted by Gayle and Caroline!

Again, we must thank Julie and Barbara for putting up with life whilst this book was being prepared. Without them it would never have happened!

AUTHORS NOTES

This book is the last in a series of three volumes charting the progress of the war in Sussex and deals with the years 1943 to VE Day in 1945. The period covered a time when the RAF and USAAF were going heavily onto the offensive with air attacks on Occupied Europe and regularly saw the skies over the county thick with formations of outgoing or returning bombers. Thus it was felt appropriate to give this book the title "*Bombers Over Sussex 1943-45*".

In addition to massed Allied air raids which processed across the county's skies the period also saw a continuation of German air attacks, including the "Hit and Run" raids which had already brought so much terror to coastal regions through 1942. Although on a diminished scale, German air activity nevertheless accounted for a heavy toll on civilian life and, in 1943, resulted in the largest loss of life in a single air raid (see East Grinstead Urban District)in the county. Perhaps the most notable feature relating to German aerial activity over Sussex during the period covered by this book was the Flying Bomb (V1) and Rocket (V2) attack period. Unleashed after the D-Day Invasion these weapons terrorised the civilian population of South East England and, lying under the direct flight path to London from launch sites in Northern France, the county of Sussex was particularly badly affected by falling V1 Flying Bombs. Over 900 fell in the county, causing widespread death and destruction - particularly in East Sussex. Defence against these weapons ranged from barage balloons, to fighter aircraft and anti-aircraft weaponry of every description. Against the V2 rocket, however, there was no defence. Mercifully, only four fell in Sussex causing relatively little damage.

Against the background of continuing German air attack, however, must be seen the D-Day Invasion of 6th June 1944. The build up to this momentous day was played out across

Southern England and, once again, Sussex was at the very forefront of preparations for invasion. Indeed, the whole county was transformed during the lead-up period into a vast armed camp. To its surprised residents, however, the county seemed to empty overnight of thousands of tanks, trucks and soldiers whilst the sky reverberated to the drone of immense aerial armadas as D-Day dawned. It was almost another year, however, before the war in Europe was finally over on VE Day, 8th May 1945. The cessation of hostilities emptied the skies of aerial activity which had, by now, become commonplace and the joy of the occasion was outwardly expressed in VE Day celebrations the length and breadth of Sussex. Over four years of warfare, however, had left its mark on the county and half a century on the scars may still be seen or felt. These three volumes present a county-wide record of some of the more significant or memorable events of those momentous years and are produced as a tribute to those who participated or suffered. They are not, however, intended to be a comprehensive record of events as such detail could not be incorporated into volumes of this size.

As with "*Battle Over Sussex 1940*" and "*Blitz Over Sussex 1941-42*" this book is laid out on a district-by-district basis, following the boundaries of rural districts, urban districts, municipal boroughs and county boroughs then in being.

Documentary material from official archives, contemporary records, eye witness accounts and a variety of other sources have all been used in the compilation of this work. Similarly, the wide range of pictures used have come from a variety of sources although it has often been difficult to trace photographs relevant to certain of the geographical areas covered in this book.

The authors would continue to be delighted to hear from anyone having new or additional information, photographs or souvenirs relating to the war in Sussex. They may be contacted via Tangmere Military Aviation Museum, Tangmere Airfield, Chichester, West Sussex, PO20 6ES.

MAPS

The maps are all based upon the 1940 edition of the Ordnance Survey of Great Britain. Four regions of the county have been selected to give a representative cover of East and West Sussex on which have been marked a proportion of the aircraft down in those areas. For clarity, not every incident in each area has necessarily been marked. Those that are shown are indicated in the exact position if known, or at a close proximation to the believed or reported position of the crash. The size of the county and the number of incidents logged in the 1943-1945 period precludes the inclusion of maps showing all of Sussex and all of the reported aircraft losses. The scale has been reduced to 0.75" to 1 mile. The numbers shown on the maps are listed in the tables on pages 92 to 95.

PHOTOGRAPHS

Every effort has been made to clear copyright but the sources of pictures used are varied and, in many cases, obscure. Some are from private collections and others from agencies and organisations no longer in existence. Therefore, the publication of any picture for which clearance has not been given is wholly unintentional. It is hoped, however, that their appearance within this book will be seen as a tribute to civilian and service personnel who died or suffered in the county of Sussex during the period 1943 to 1945.

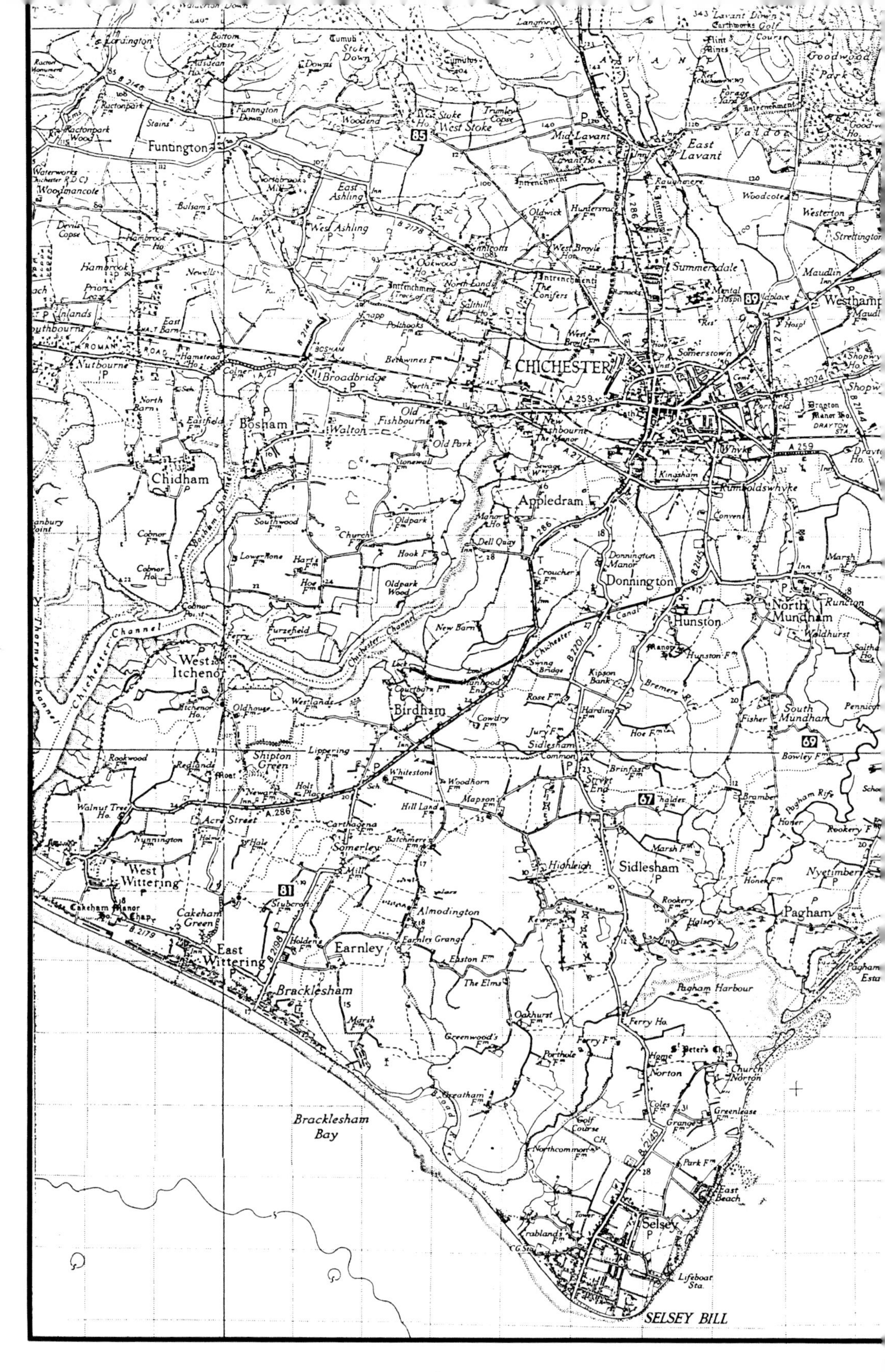

Lordington
Bottom Copse
Stoke Down
Racton Monument
Adsdean Ho.
Goodwood Park
Flint Mines
Funtington
Ructonpark Wood
Stains
Funnyngton Down
Woodend
West Stoke
Trumley Copse
Mid Lavant
East Lavant
Lavant Ho.
Valdoe
Waterworks
Woodmancote
Intrenchment
Raughmere
Woodcote
East Ashling
Westerton
Bulsam's Fm
Oldwick Fm
Huntersrace
Devils Copse
Hambrook Ho.
West Ashling
B 2178
Strettington
Hambrook
Newells
Oakwood Ho.
West Broyle Ho.
Summersdale
Maudlin
North Lands
The Conifers
Mental Hospl
Westhampnett
Priors Leaze
Salthill Ho.
Inlands
Knapp
Polthooks Fm
Southbourne
East Barn
ROMAN ROAD
Hamstead Ho.
Nutbourne
Bethwines Fm
CHICHESTER
Somerstown
Colner Fm
Broadbridge
Bosham Sta.
Shopwyke
A.259
A 2024
North Barn
Eastfield Fm
Bosham
Walton
Old Fishbourne
New Fishbourne
The Manor
Portfield
Drayton Manor Ho.
Drayton Sta.
Old Park
Whyke
A 259
Stonewall Fm
Chidham
Kingsham
Rumboldswhyke
Appledram
Sewage Wks
Southwood Fm
Manor Ho.
Convent
Church Fm
Oldpark Fm
Cobnor Fm
Bosham Channel
Lower Rone Fm
Harts Fm
Hook Fm
Dell Quay
Donnington Manor
Croucher Fm
Cobnor Ho.
Hoe Fm
Oldpark Wood
Donnington
Marsh Fm
Runcton
Cobnor Point
Canal
Hunston
North Mundham
Channel
Furzefield
New Barn
Waldhurst
Ferry
Chichester Channel
Hunston Fm
West Itchenor
Manor
Swing Bridge
Kipson Bank
Chichester Channel
Thorney Channel
Courtbarn Fm
Hunwood End
Rose Fm
Bremere Rife
Westlands Fm
Itchenor Ho.
Oldhouse Fm
Birdham
Cowdry Fm
Harding
South Mundham
Fisher
Pennicott
Jury Fm
Sidlesham Common
Hoe Fm
Bowley Fm
Rookwood Fm
Redlands
Shipton Green
Lippering Fm
Whitestone
Brinfast Fm
Street End
Woodhorn Fm
Holt Place
Newark Fm
Mapson's Fm
Chalder Fm
Bramber Fm
Pagham Rife
Walnut Tree Ho.
Acre Street
A.286
Hill Land Fm
Carthagena Fm
Rookery Fm
Honer
Nunnington Fm
Holme Fm
Hale Fm
Batchmere's Fm
Somerley
Marsh Fm
Highleigh
Nyetimber
West Wittering
Mill Fm
Sidlesham
Honer Fm
Stubcroft Fm
Almodington
Rookery Fm
Pagham
Cakeham Manor
Cakeham Green
Keynor Fm
Halsey Fm
B.2179
Holden's Fm
Earnley
Earnley Grange
East Wittering
B 2198
Ebston Fm
Pagham Esta.
Bracklesham
The Elms
Pagham Harbour
Oakhurst Fm
Ferry Ho.
Marsh Fm
Ferry Fm
Greenwood's Fm
Porthole Fm
St. Peter's Ch.
Home
Norton
Church Norton
Greatham Fm
Coles Fm
Greenlease Fm
Bracklesham Bay
Grange Fm
Golf Course
B 2145
Northcommon Fm
Park Fm
East Beach
Tower
Selsey
Crablands
C.G. Sta.
Lifeboat Sta.
SELSEY BILL

Map A

RAF ORGANISATION

Whilst the organisation of RAF operational units into Squadrons will no doubt be familiar to most readers, it is perhaps worth explaining that each Squadron comprised roughly about twelve aircraft and a corresponding number of pilots or aircrew. Clearly this number was subject to fluctuation depending upon serviceable aircraft and losses of pilots or machines. A Squadron could often be depleted to below strength pending the replacement of men or machines. However, the Battle Order of the RAF can be found elsewhere in other reference works, although it is worth mentioning here that the entire County of Sussex fell within the defence region of No. 11 Group, RAF Fighter Command.

US ARMY AIR FORCE AND ROYAL AIR FORCE RANK EQUIVALENTS

USAAF	RAF
General of the AF	Marshal of the RAF
General	Air Chief Marshal
Lt General	Air Marshal
Major General	Air Vice Marshal
Brig. General	Air Commodore
Colonel	Group Captain
Lt Colonel	Wing Commander
Major	Squadron Leader
Captain	Flight Lieutenant
Lieutenant	Flying Officer
Second Lt	Pilot Officer

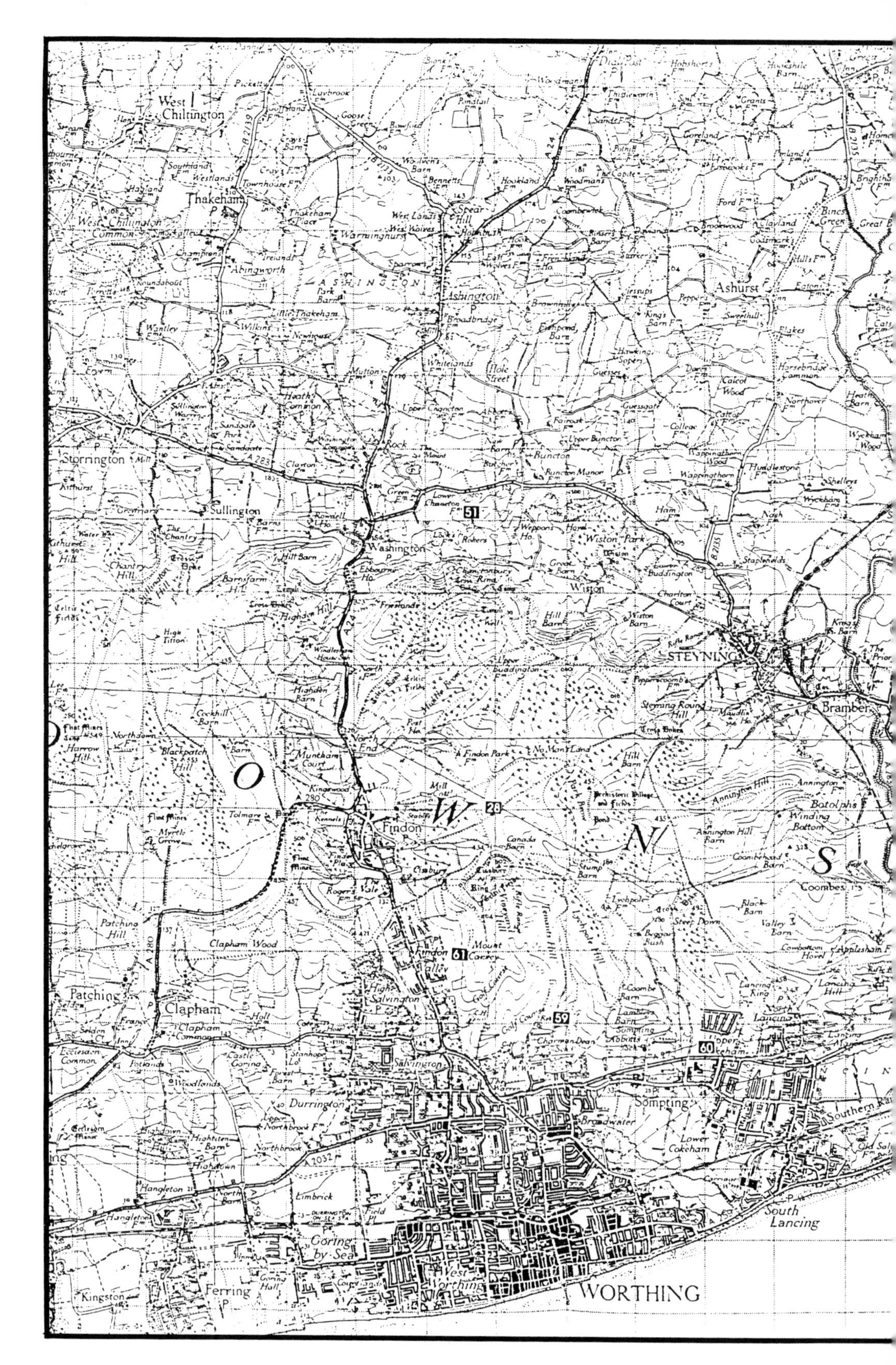
West Chiltington
Thakeham
West Chiltington Common
Abingworth
ASHINGTON
Ashington
Spear Hill
Broadbridge
Storrington
Sullington
Washington
Chanctonbury Ring
Wiston
Wiston Park
Ashurst
Bines Green
Buncton
STEYNING
Bramber
Botolphs
Findon
Cissbury Ring
Findon Valley
High Salvington
Salvington
Durrington
Patching
Clapham
Clapham Wood
Sompting
Broadwater
Lancing
South Lancing
Goring by Sea
West Worthing
WORTHING
Ferring
Kingston
Hangleton
Highdown
Coombes
D
O
W
N
S
51
28
61
59
60

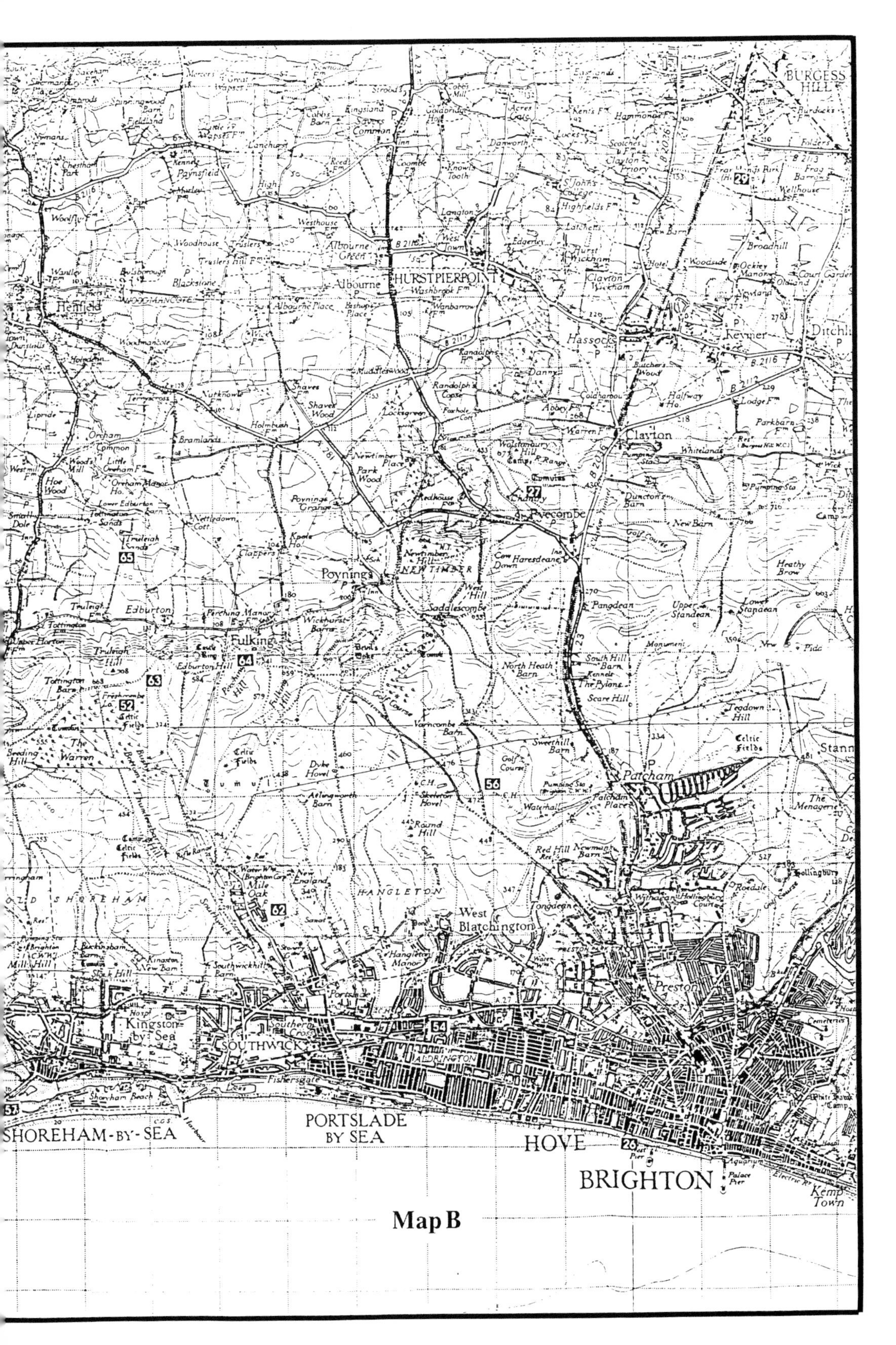
BURGESS HILL
HURSTPIERPOINT
Albourne
Henfield
Hassocks
Keymer
Ditchling
Clayton
Pyecombe
Poynings
Fulking
Edburton
Saddlescombe
Patcham
West Blatchington
HANGLETON
OLD SHOREHAM
Preston
Kingston by Sea
SOUTHWICK
ALDRINGTON
Fishersgate
Shoreham Beach
SHOREHAM-BY-SEA
PORTSLADE BY SEA
HOVE
BRIGHTON
Kemp Town

Map B

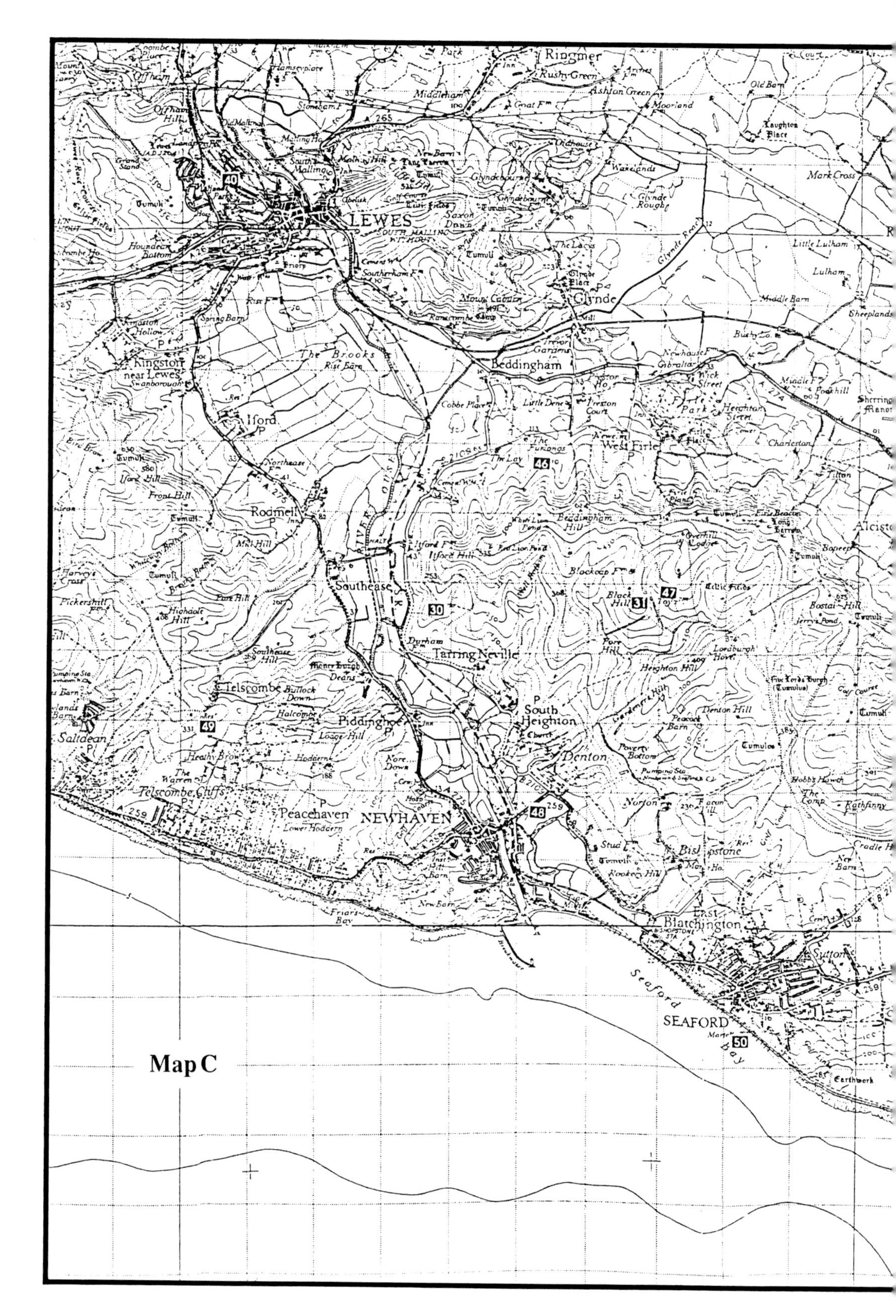
Ringmer
Rushy Green
Ashton Green
Moorland
Old Barn
Laughton Place
Middleham
Stoneham Fm
Offham
Offham Hill
Old Malling
Malling Ho
South Malling
Mark Cross
Wakelands
Glyndebourne
Glynde Rough
Grand Stand
Tumuli
LEWES
Saxon Down
Little Lulham
Lulham
The Lacys
Glynde Place
Glynde
Glynde Reach
Southerham Fm
Mount Caburn
Ranscombe Camp
Middle Barn
Sheeplands
Houndean Bottom
Priory
Kingston Hollow
Spring Barn
Kingston near Lewes
Swanborough
The Brooks
Rise Barn
Beddingham
Trevor Gardens
Newhouse Fm
Gibraltar
Wick Street
Firle Park
Heighton Street
Bushy Co.
Preston Court
Little Dene
Cobbe Place
Iford
West Firle
Firle Place
Charleston
Tilton
The Furlongs
The Lay
Northease Fm
Iford Hill
Front Hill
Rodmell
Beddingham Hill
Firle Beacon
Alciston
Bopeep
Mill Hill
Itford Fm
Itford Hill
Blackcap Fm
Southease
Black Hill
Celtic Fields
Bostal Hill
Jerry's Pond
Harvey's Cross
Pickershill Fm
Highdole Hill
Park Hill
Durham
Tarring Neville
Southease Hill
Heighton Hill
Lordburgh Hove
Telscombe
Bullock Down
Deans
Halcombe
Saltdean
Piddinghoe
Lodge Hill
South Heighton
Denton Hill
Denton
Heathy Brow
Hoddern
Nore Down
Poverty Bottom
Hobbs Hawth
Telscombe Cliffs
The Warren
Norton
Rathfinny
Peacehaven
Lower Hoddern
NEWHAVEN
Bishopstone
Cradle Hill
Rookery Hill
New Barn
Friars Bay
East Blatchington
Sutton
Seaford Bay
SEAFORD
Earthwork
River Ouse
A 26
A 275
A 274
A 259
B 2109
40
46
30
31
47
49
48
50

Map C

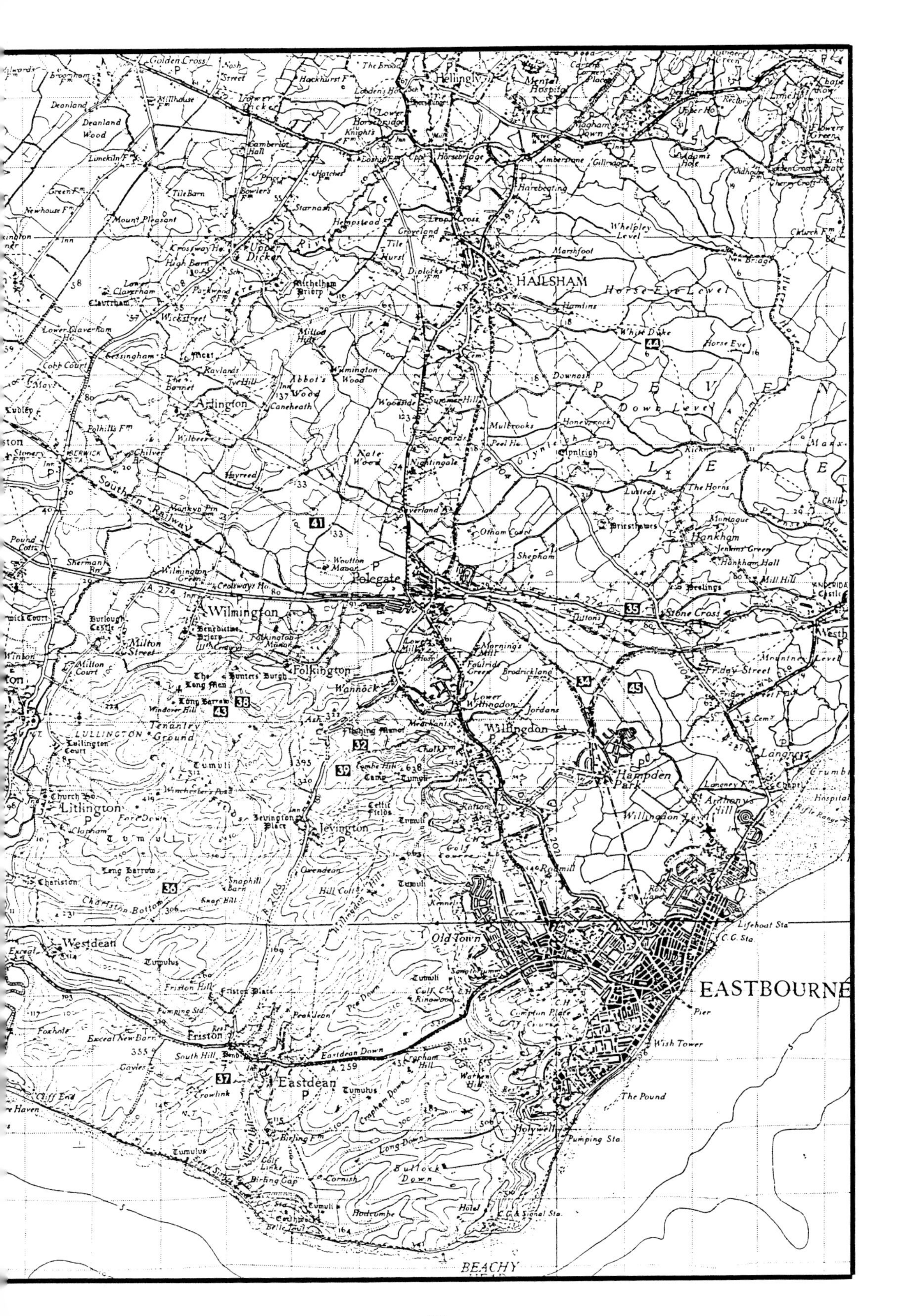

Golden Cross
Hellingly
Mental Hospital
Deanland Wood
Lower Horsebridge
Horsebridge
Amberstone
Magham Down
Harebeating
Hempstead
Trap Cross
Upper Dicker
Michelham Priory
HAILSHAM
Horse Eye Level
Whelpley Level
Marshfoot
Hamlins
White Duke
Horse Eye
Downash
PEVENSEY LEVEL
Arlington
Abbot's Wood
Wilmington Wood
Summer Hill
Mulbrooks
Glynleigh
Southern Railway
Priesthawes
Hankham
Hankham Hall
Otham Court
Shepham
Polegate
Wootton Manor
Wilmington
Stone Cross
Folkington
Wannock
Milton Street
Lullington Court
Long Man
Windover Hill
Willingdon
Hampden Park
Willingdon Level
St. Anthony's Hill
Langney
Jevington
Litlington
Charleston
Westdean
Friston
Friston Hill
Eastdean
Old Town
EASTBOURNE
Pier
Wish Tower
The Pound
Holywell
Pumping Sta.
Birling Gap
Crowlink
Cliff End
Bullock Down
Long Down
Hodcombe
Belle Tout
BEACHY HEAD

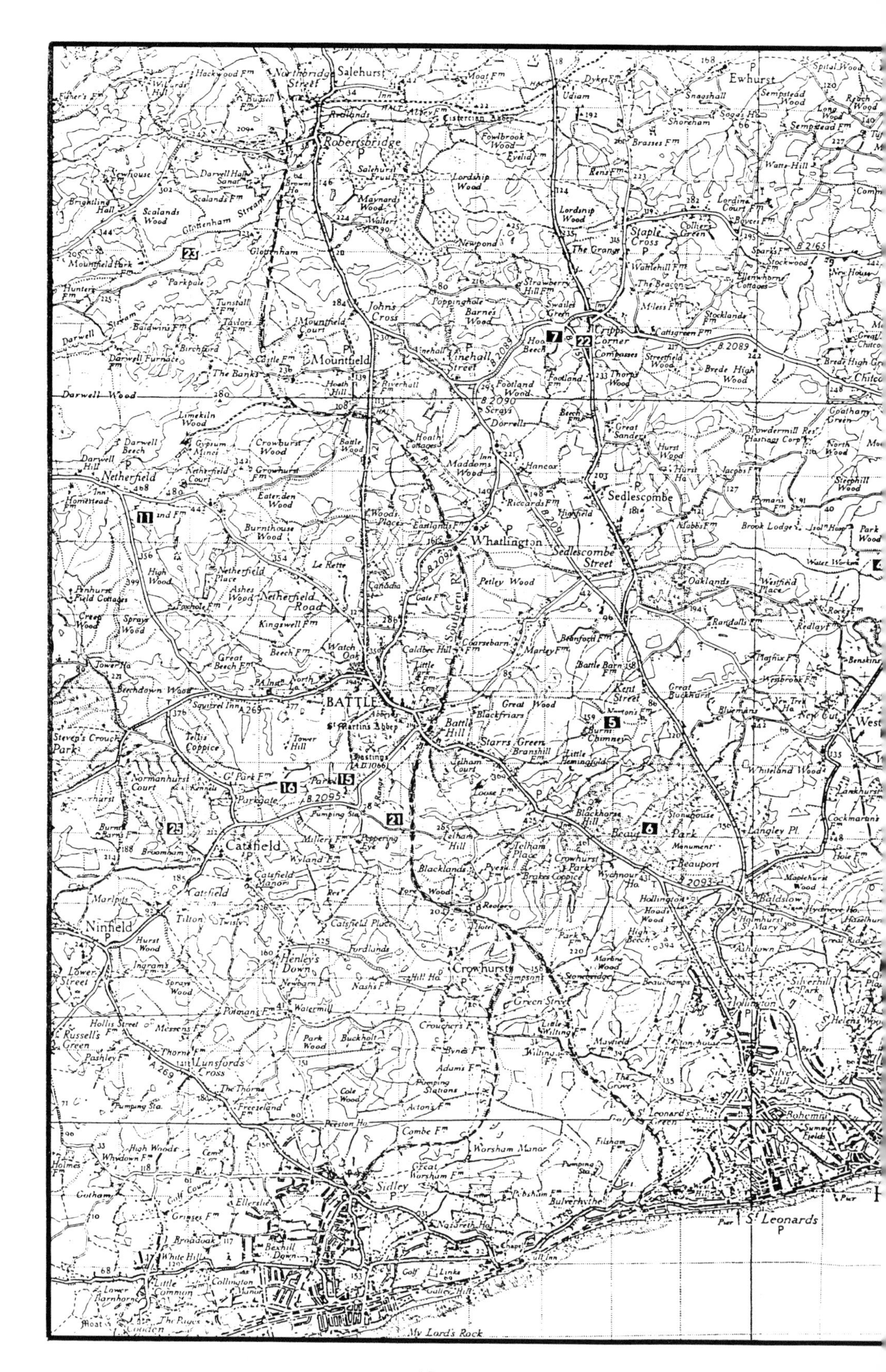

Salehurst
Northbridge Street
Robertsbridge
Cistercian Abbey
Ewhurst
Udiam
Sempstead Wood
Fowlbrook Wood
Lordship Wood
Salehurst Fruit Fm
Maynards Wood
Darwell Hall Sanat
Scalands Fm
Scalands Wood
Brightling Hall
Glottenham Stream
Glottenham
Mountfield Park Fm
Newpond
The Grange
Staple Cross
Colliers Green
Bream Fm
Parkpale
Tunstall Fm
Taylors Fm
Baldwins Fm
Birchford
Darwell
Darwell Furnace
Castle Fm
Mountfield
Mountfield Court
Johns Cross
Poppinghole
Barnes Wood
Vinehall Street
Strawberry Hill Fm
Swailes Green
Cripps Corner
Compasses
Hoo Beech
Footland Wood
Thorny Wood
Streetfield Wood
Brede High Wood
B.2089
The Banks
Darwell Wood
Limekiln Wood
Riverhall Fm
Heath Hill
B.2090
Scrays
Dorrells
Darwell Beech
Gypsum Mines
Crowhurst Wood
Battle Wood
Heath Cottages
Maddoms Wood
Great Sanders
Hurst Wood
Powdermill Res
Darwell Hill
Netherfield
Netherfield Court
Growhurst Fm
Eatenden Wood
Hancox
Riccards Fm
Sedlescombe
Burnthouse Wood
Woods Place
Eastlands Fm
Whatlington
Sedlescombe Street
High Wood
Netherfield Place
Le Rette
Ashes Wood
Netherfield Road
Canadia
Gate Fm
B.2092
Southern Ry
Petley Wood
Oaklands
Westfield Place
Penhurst Field Cottages
Creep Wood
Sprays Wood
Kingswell Fm
Caldbec Hill
Coarsebarn Fm
Marley Fm
Beanfort Fm
Randalls Fm
Great Beech Fm
Beech Fm
Watch Oak
Battle Barn Fm
Kent Street
Great Buckhurst
Tower Ha
Beechdown Wood
Squirrel Inn
A.265
BATTLE
Abbey
St Martins Abbey
Battle Hill
Great Wood
Blackfriars
Starrs Green
Branshill Fm
Burnt Chimney
Little Hemingfold
Steven's Crouch
Park
Tellis Coppice
Tower Hill
Hastings (A.D.1066)
Telham Court
Normanhurst Court
Gt Park Fm
Park
Purkgate
B.2095
Pumping Sta
Rifle Range
Loose Fm
Blackhorse Hill
Beauport Park
Stonehouse
Langley Pl
Catsfield
Broomham
Millers Fm
Peppering Eye
Wyland Fm
Telham Hill
Telham Place
Crowhurst Park
Monument
Beauport
Catsfield Manor
Blacklands
Brakes Coppice
Wychnour Ho
B.2093
Baldslow
Marlpits
Catsfield
Fore Wood
Reclory
Hollington
Ninfield
Tilton
Twisly
Catsfield Place
Hotel
High Beech
Holmhurst St Mary
Hurst Wood
Henley's Down
Fordlands
Park Fm
Ingrams
Crowhurst
Sampsons
Stonebridge
Marline Wood
Beauchamps
Lower Street
Sprays Wood
Newbarn Fm
Nashs Fm
Hill Ha
Green Street
Silverhill Park
Potmans Fm
Watermill
Hollington
Hollis Street
Messens Fm
Crouchers Fm
Little Wilting Fm
Russell's Green
Park Wood
Buckholt Fm
Byne Fm
Wilting Fm
Maxfield Fm
Pashley Fm
Thorne Fm
Lunsfords Cross
Adams Fm
The Grove
Silver Hill
A.269
The Thorne
Cole Wood
Pumping Stations
Pumping Sta
Freezeland Fm
Actons Fm
St Leonard's Green
Bohemia
Preston Ho
Combe Fm
Worsham Manor
Filsham
Summer Fields
High Woods
Whydown Fm
Cem
Great Worsham Fm
Pumping Sta
Holmes
Golf Course
Sidley
Gotham
Ellerslie
Pebsham Fm
Bulverhythe
Grisses Fm
Naisreth Ho
St Leonards
Pier
Broadoak
Bexhill Down
Chapel
White Hill
Golf Links
Little Common
Collington Manor
Gulley Hill
Lower Barnhorne
Moat
The Ridges
Cooden
My Lord's Rock
23
7
22
11
16
15
21
25
5
6

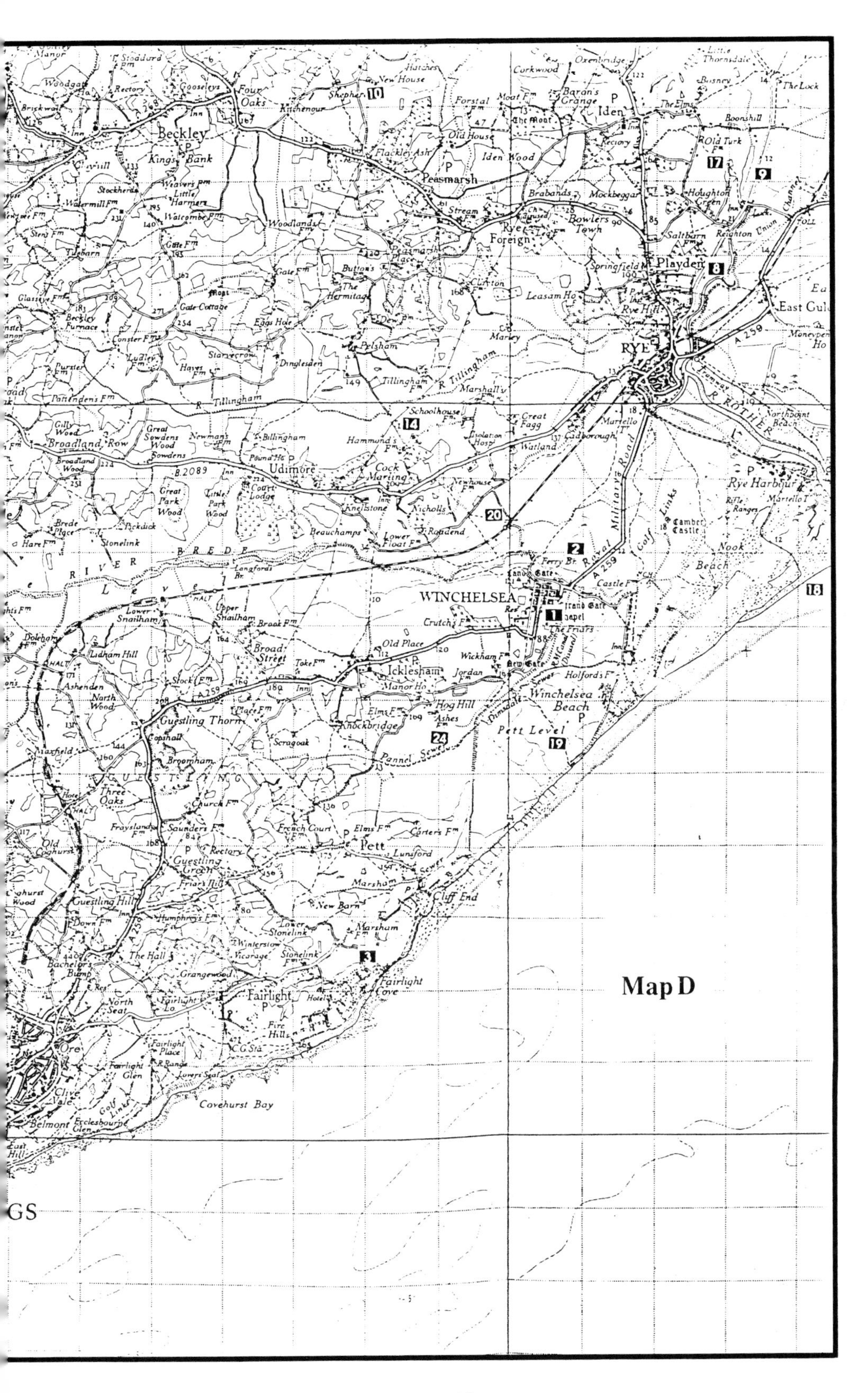

Map D
Beckley
Four Oaks
Kings Bank
Peasmarsh
Flackley Ash
Old House
Iden Wood
Iden
Corkwood
Oxenbridge
Baran's Grange
The Moat
Boonshill
Old Turk Fm
Houghton Green
Saltbarn
Playden
Rye Foreign
Bowlers Town
Mockbeggar
Brabands
Leasam Ho
Rye Hill
RYE
East Guldeford
A 259
R Rother
Tramway
Woodlands Fm
Peasmarsh Place
The Hermitage
Clifton
Marley
Pelsham
Tillingham Fm
R Tillingham
Marshall's
Dinglesden
Starvecrow
Hayes Fm
Gate Cottage
Beckley Furnace
Conster Fm
Pattenden's Fm
Schoolhouse Fm
Great Fagg
Cadborough
Martello
Royal Military Road
Golf Links
Camber Castle
Rye Harbour
Rifle Ranges
Nook Beach
Hammond's Fm
Isolation Hospl
Watland
Udimore
Cock Marling
Newhouse Fm
Nicholls
Knellstone
Broadland Row
Broadland Wood
Great Sowdens Wood
Newman's Fm
Billingham
B.2089
Court Lodge
Great Park Wood
Little Park Wood
Brede Place
Stonelink
Beauchamps
Lower Float Fm
Roundend
Ferry Br.
R. BREDE
RIVER
Level
Langfords Br.
WINCHELSEA
The Friars
Castle Fm
Crutch's Fm
Lower Snailham
Upper Snailham
Brook Fm
Broad Street
Old Place
Icklesham
Manor Ho
Wickham Fm
Jordan
Holford's Fm
Winchelsea Beach
Pett Level
Hog Hill
Ashes Fm
Knockbridge
Elms Fm
Toke Fm
Lidham Hill
Ashenden
North Wood
Guestling Thorn
Place Fm
Scragoak
Pannel Sewer
Broomham
Three Oaks
Church Fm
Saunders Fm
Fraysland Fm
Old Coghurst
Rectory
Guestling Green
Friars Hill
French Court
Pett
Elms Fm
Carters Fm
Lunsford
Marsham
Cliff End
New Barn
Guestling Hill
Humphrey's Fm
Down Fm
Lower Stonelink
Marsham Fm
The Hall
Wintersto
Vicarage
Stonelink Fm
Bachelor's Bump
Grangewood
Fairlight
Fairlight Cove
Hotel
North Seat
Fire Hills
C.G.Sta
Ore
Fairlight Place
Fairlight Glen
Lovers' Seat
Clive Vale
Golf Links
Covehurst Bay
Belmont
Ecclesbourne Glen
East Hill
GS

ARUNDEL MUNICIPAL BOROUGH

The close proximity of RAF Ford inevitably resulted in intense aerial activity above Arundel as aircraft took off or joined the landing circuit for the airfield. On 10th February 1943, a Ford based Beaufighter of 141 Squadron overshot its landing and in a steep turn hit a wooded hillside near the Black Rabbit Inn. Flying Officer Kahn, Sgt. P. Nockles and Sgt. J. Price were all killed as the aeroplane disintegrated on impact with a sturdy beech tree and until the storms of October, 1987, the gaunt limbless trunk still stood to mark the scene of tragedy. Kahn, an Indian, was buried by arrangement with India House at Brookwood Mohammedan Cemetery.

During the early hours of 8th March a raider dropped a string of five bombs across the district but, by great good fortune, Arundel's luck in escaping any civilian injury across four years of war was to continue. Indeed, no damage or casualties were caused by these bombs which fell near the Black Rabbit, in a field on the Warningcamp Road and in open country at South Stoke.

On the 13th May, Flt. Lt. Reg Baker of 182 Squadron struggled back across the Channel in his Typhoon which had been badly holed by flak south of Berck and managed to crash-land his stricken fighter at Ford Junction, Arundel, writing off the aeroplane in the process. Lucky to escape this episode Baker was hit by flak and killed almost exactly one year later.

There followed a lull of a year before any further aircraft losses occurred in the district when, on 22nd June 1944, a four engined B-24 Liberator of the USAAF dived vertically to earth at Park Farm, Arundel. Hit by anti-aircraft fire over Normandy the crippled bomber made the English coast before most of the crew baled out. Still on board were the pilot and co-pilot who both died in the crash which drove much of the wreckage sixteen feet underground. By a strange quirk of fate there may well have been a distant connection between the pilot, 1st Lt. William B. Montgomery, and the founder of Arundel Castle on which estate Park Farm lies. Roger de Montgomery built the castle at the end of the 11th century. Could he have been one of William B. Montgomery's ancestors? Whilst this makes for some interesting speculation the horrific reality of the crash was fully exposed in 1974 with the recovery of the wrecked bomber from beneath grazing land. Mangled beyond any recognition, the bomber's wreckage contained two grim looking coffin-like armoured seats in which Montgomery and his co-pilot had ridden to their death as they held the bomber steady for the crew to escape. Of both men there was simply no trace beyond tiny charred shreds of parachute material. Classified as "Missing In Action" the men are commemorated by name on The Wall of The Missing at Madingley American Cemetery, Cambridge.

With the coming of VE Day in May 1945, the townsfolk of Arundel, though not untouched by this war, could rejoice in the fact that not one of its residents had been killed by enemy action. Nevertheless, like all communities, there were many families who had loved ones who would not be returning from active service at the cessation of hostilities.

1. The Wall of The Missing at Maddingley American Cemetery, Cambridge, is the only memorial to the pilot of a B-24 Liberator which crashed at Arundel on 22nd June 1944. Ist Lt. William B. Montgomery's name may be found there with thousands of others.

MITCHINER GEORGE R · 2 LT · 511 SQ 405 FTR BOMBER GP · CALIFORNIA
MJELLEM MARTIN L · 2 LT · 364 BOMB SQ 305 BOMB GP(H) · CALIFORNIA
MOAK CARL G · S SGT · 526 BOMB SQ 379 BOMB GP(H) · ILLINOIS
MODAFFERI LOUIS D · T SGT · 325 BOMB SQ 92 BOMB GP(H) · NEW YORK
MOERBE EDWARD E · 2 LT · 561 BOMB SQ 388 BOMB GP(H) · TEXAS
MOKE FRANCIS E · 2 LT · 838 BOMB SQ 487 BOMB GP(H) · MISSOURI
MOLANDER NORMAN C · · PFC · · 306 QM BN · · FLORIDA
MOLANS JOHN J · S SGT · 568 BOMB SQ 390 BOMB GP(H) · CONNECTICUT
MOLINARI JOSEPH J · S SGT · 561 BOMB SQ 388 BOMB GP(H) · NEW YORK
MOLLOHAN WILLIAM L JR · SGT · 2 RANGER BN · WEST VIRGINIA
MOLNAR STEVE · T SGT · 561 BOMB SQ 388 BOMB GP(H) · OHIO
MONAHAN WILLIAM J · 1 LT · 858 BOMB SQ 492 BOMB GP(H) · MASSACHUSETTS
MONIER FERDINAND A JR · CPL · 388 BOMB SQ 96 BOMB GP(H) · TEXAS
MONTGOMERY WILLIAM B · 1 LT · 844 BOMB SQ 489 BOMB GP(H) · PA
MONTGOMERY WILLIAM J · 2 LT · 325 BOMB SQ 92 BOMB GP(H) · TEXAS
MOODY EDWARD B · · SGT · · 175 FA BN 34 DIV · · MINNESOTA
MOODY JACK E · S SGT · 90 SQ 438 TRP CARR GP · NEW YORK
MOONEY WILLIAM R · S SGT · 614 BOMB SQ 401 BOMB GP(H) · ARKANSAS
MOOR JAMES W · 2 LT · 577 BOMB SQ 392 BOMB GP(H) · TEXAS
MOORE HUGH L · 1 LT · 413 BOMB SQ 96 BOMB GP(H) · GEORGIA
MOORE JOHN F · T SGT · 535 BOMB SQ 381 BOMB GP(H) · NEW JERSEY
MOORE JOHN H · SGT · 577 BOMB SQ 392 BOMB GP(H) · NORTH CAROLINA
MOORE PAUL R · S SGT · 751 BOMB SQ 457 BOMB GP(H) · MARYLAND

BATTLE RURAL DISTRICT

On the 4th January 1943, two enemy raiders came to grief in Battle Rural District within a few miles of each other. The first was a low - flying Focke Wulf 190 which collided with overhead cables and crashed at Castle Farm, Winchelsea, spreading the disintegrating wreckage over a wide area and killing its pilot, Fw Muller. Later that evening a Dornier 217 came in at low level from the sea at Fairlight and, in bad visibility, flew into the rising ground at Furze Hill. The bomber smashed through an empty bungalow and broke up, leaving only the rear fuselage, tail and engines relatively intact. In the incident all four crew were killed and, unusually, they were all taken along with the body of the Focke Wulf pilot to Folkestone for burial. (Normally it was the practice to bury dead German aircrew close to the town or village where they had fallen.) At the Fairlight incident, local residents sat proudly on what they thought was a fuel tank from the German bomber and posed happily for photographs - not realising it was an unexploded parachute mine!

Battle Abbey (and Battle itself!) had a remarkable escape on 2nd February when three fighter bombers released bombs on the town and one of them bounced off the Abbey Green into the gateway of the Abbey where it smashed to pieces but did not explode. A sentry on duty there was injured in the leg by the disintegrating bomb but if it had detonated the results may well have been catastrophic because in that building Royal Engineers stored two tons of gelignite for demolition purposes. Further along the High Street, another bomb fell behind the George Hotel and failed to explode, although the third detonated, destroyed two shops and killed Tom and Gladys Giles at No.75. It was thought locally that the raiders were aiming for the Newberry Jam Factory, although it is possible they had no specific aiming point at all. However, the strange behaviour of bombs when they bounced or fell flat and failed to explode is explained by the fact that they had been released at ultra-low level. There were many similar cases of "bouncing bombs", particularly during the low altitude fighter bomber attacks.

These attacks continued with Winchelsea the next to be bombed on 13th February when Salutation Cottages were hit, killing Violet Morris. Attacks of this nature gradually declined throughout 1943, although an isolated incident at Burwash on 11th August claimed the life of an 18 year old ATC Cadet, John Aspin, but it is not clear if his death was directly attributable to enemy air attack or through other "war causes".

There continued a steadily rising toll of Allied aircraft down in the district, and in 1943 alone at least 16 losses occurred.

On 29th August, for example, an RAF Mustang of 231 Squadron returning from patrol in bad weather hit an obstruction on high ground and crashed at Marley Lane. However, just as the year had begun, it ended with the loss of a German aircraft. This time it was a Messerschmitt 410 which had been shot down by a Mosquito on the night of 19th/20th December to crash at Boonshill Farm, Playden. The pilot, Lt. Baack, was killed but Uffz. Strasser baled out sustaining a broken leg and being taken prisoner.

Into 1944 and yet again it was a German loss which opened the year when a Focke Wulf 190 was sent flaming onto Camber Sands on the night of 2nd/3rd January. The identity of the pilot remain uncertain, as only a rank tab for a Luffwaffe Leutnant was found but on that night a Ltn. Krakhoffer and a Ltn. Stein were both missing.

On 30th January 1944, Flt. Sgt. Henri Limet - a Belgian serving with 349 Squadron - had to bale out of his Spitfire over Battle when its engine failed. He landed unhurt and the Spitfire crashed at Ironbridge, Telham Lane. A recent investigation of the crash site revealed the propeller hub still buried there and this led to research attempting to trace Limet. It was found that he had been shot down and taken prisoner on 28th April 1944. Although safely repatriated on 10th May 1945, he was later to die as a crewmember of a Belgian SABENA aircraft that crashed in the Belgian Congo during 1948. Other searches for surviving aircrew have had happier outcomes as will be seen later.

Allied aircraft losses were again heavy during 1944, and at least 40 were recorded as having crashed in that time in the Battle Rural District. D-Day on 6th June, however, at least offered some hope that an end to it all was in sight but, in the early morning of that momentous day, two USAAF B-26 Marauders collided over the district. As huge formations of planes formed up to head out to Normandy one of the B-26 aircraft iced up at high altitude and spun down out of control. As it fell, it struck another B-26 in a lower formation and both aeroplanes crashed - one at Ashburnham Park the other at Ringletts Farm, Whatlington. The bombs on board which had been destined for German coastal gun batteries at Varreville exploded violently, only one man from the two crews having escaped by parachute. Extensive damage was done to Ashburnham Place and the estate houses and a huge crater ripped in woodland. Until the storms of 1987, large panels from the disintegrated bomber hung high up in the branches of tall beech trees - themselves scarred by blast and shrapnel impacts.

When it came, the Flying Bomb campaign brought no less than 374 of these weapons crashing to earth and exploding in the Rural District. For such a large number it seems remarkable that there were not more than three fatal casualties caused to the civilian population as a result. There was, though, a considerable loss of property. At Ticehurst, however, one fell without exploding and enabled investigators to remove and examine the warhead - the first example to be recovered intact from a V1.

In defending the British Isles against V1 attacks RAF Fighter Command lost a considerable number of aircraft and pilots, and at the height of the Campaign in July at least six Tempests on "Anti Diver" patrols were lost in the area. Flying Officer George Kosh of 3 Squadron died at Winchelsea on lst July, whilst not far away at Playden on the 3rd one of his Squadron colleagues, Flt. Sgt. Stanislaw Domanski of Poland, died at Cliff Farm. In his pocket was his Marriage Certificate, and having just married a young Scottish girl he was taken to Falkirk for burial.

At night the patrols by fighter aircraft continued as they chased the flaming tails of "Doodlebugs" across the sky. On 18th July, a Mosquito and Tempest on V1 night patrol collided, the Mosquito crashing at Boarders Farm, Etchingham, killing Flt. Sgt. Hoare and Flt. Sgt. Bishop. The Tempest crashed in Hailsham Rural District at Broad Oak, Heathfield, Wing Commander Hartley baling out and surviving.

In contrast, an American pilot had a truly remarkable escape at Iden Lock on 16th July. Bob Benton of the 22nd Fighter Squadron, 36th Fighter Group, takes up his own story:-

"At 18.30 hrs we took off from Kingsnorth for a dive-bombing and straffing mission on a railway marshalling yard at Nantes, France, and flew across at ground level to avoid radar. Half way to target we ran into intense flak and my aeroplane was hit and caught fire but I dropped my auxiliary wing tanks and that put out the fire. I completed the mission successfully but on my return across France my 'plane started running rough. Thank God we made it across the Channel, but as soon as we crossed over the English coast my engine got rougher then stopped completely. I pulled up to gain some altitude and to look for a crash-landing spot. It was almost 22.30 hrs and getting dark. I could see it was not a good place to crash land so decided to bale out. I was losing air speed and altitude fast so opened the canopy and pushed the nose of the 'plane down to propel me out. Unfortunately, my right foot caught in the cockpit and although they always say never pull the ripcord when still attached to the 'plane I knew I was dead unless I did. The ground was coming up fast and I was still trapped. Then I pulled the ripcord, the parachute opened and pulled me from the Thunderbolt. To this day I don't remember floating down even for just one second, and I must have been knocked out on landing. When I woke I heard people shouting and running towards me. Looking for my 'plane I saw just the tail section sticking out of the water of a nearby canal and had been pulled clear by my parachute at the last moment".

In July 1994, fifty years exactly after his miraculous escape, Bob Benton returned with his family to revisit the area where he had come so very close to death.

The last aircraft down in 1944 was a returning battle-damaged Lancaster of 44 Squadron which fell at Silverhill, Hurst Green, on lst November. Before they baled out the crew had the sad task of dropping out of the aircraft the body of their Captain who had been killed over enemy territory. No doubt they felt this was preferable to leaving the unfortunate young man in the doomed bomber.

The year drew to a close with a bang as, on 28th November at 23.35 hrs, a V2 rocket exploded over Burwash. Although the blast caused damage to a number of properties - some of it extensive - no casualties were recorded.

On 28th March 1945, a 303 Bomb Group B-17 Flying Fortress of the USAAF crash landed on the foreshore at Rye Harbour returning damaged from a daylight raid on Germany. The last aeroplane incident was at Sedlescombe on 6th April when a Mustang fighter was abandoned by its pilot.

At the end of it all there had been 25 civilian fatalities in 989 incidents which arose out of 2,472 alerts. At least 166 properties had been destroyed and over 8,000 properties damaged. Not since 1066 had the region seen such momentous and historically significant military action, although the cost of ensuring a rather different outcome had certainly been a heavy one.

2. The grisly scene of scattered wreckage and bodies of German airmen after a Dornier 217 had crashed at Fairlight on 4th January 1943.

488 SQUADRON. INTELLIGENCE FORM "F" AND PERSONAL COMBAT REPORT. SECRET

From:- R.A.F. Station, Bradwell Bay. Serial 488/7

To:- A.D.G.B.(2), H.Q. 11 Group (2), North Weald, Trimley, Sandwich.

STATISTICAL.

DATE.	(A)	20th December, 1943.
UNIT.	(B)	488 (N.Z.) SQUADRON.
TYPE AND MARK OF OUR AIRCRAFT.	(C)	MOSQUITO X111. AI Mk VIII.
TIME ATTACK WAS DELIVERED.	(D)	0240 hrs 20/12/43.
PLACE OF ATTACK.	(E)	Near RYE. Sussex.
WEATHER.	(F)	Good. Half Moon. Excellent Vis.
OUR CASUALTIES. AIRCRAFT.	(G)	NIL.
OUR CASUALTIES. PERSONNEL.	(H)	NIL.
ENEMY CASUALTIES IN AIR COMBAT.	(J)	One ME 410 DESTROYED.
ENEMY CASUALTIES GROUND OR SEA TARGET.	(K)	NIL.

PILOT. P/O D.N.ROBINSON. (NZ) NAV/R. F/O. W.T.M. CLARK DFM.

One Mosquito X111, AI Mk VIII, airborne 0005 hours landed Bradwell Bay 0310 patrolling under Trimley Heath G.C.I. control was warned of possible activity and ordered to climb to 15,000 feet, being taken over by Sandwich G.C.I. (Controller F/Lt KIRBY). Pilot was given several vectors but was unable to make contact with a bandit so was then given vectors on to another e/a, climbing to 21,000 feet. A contact was obtained at twelve o'clock, range 2 miles with the e/a well above so Pilot climbed to 25,000 feet and obtained a visual on an ME 410, 2000 feet ahead and slightly below. Speed of e/a approx 300 mph.

Pilot closed to 250 yards and opened fire with a 2/3 second burst but owing to vapour trails no strikes were seen. The e/a took violent evasive action, climbing and diving in tight turns but the searchlights illuminated and held the e/a and our Pilot plainly saw the black crosses on the wings. A second attack was made from 150 yards closing to 100 yards, several short bursts during which strikes were seen on the port engine and fuselage a red glow appearing from the engine. Inaccurate tracer from the barbettes was passing above our aircraft and Pilot made his third attack from 100 yards with a 2 second burst and pieces flew off the e/a which then did steep port turn and dived towards the ground. The visual was temporarily lost but the aircraft was seen to hit the ground and explode shortly afterwards.

Pilot states that prior to first attack he was above and starboard of e/a and to escape illumination and possible sighting by e/a he did very steep turn to port, thus bringing himself just above and slightly to port of the ME 410 which was well held by searchlights from the port beam and he feels his first attack was made before the e/a knew our fighter was in the vicinity.

AMMUNITION. 174 rounds each Cannon SAP/HE equal. No stoppages.
CINE GUN. (i) Yes, (ii) 0-15 degrees. (iii) One Ring (iv) 300 mph.

D Robinson
Pilot Officer.
"A" Flight,
488(N.Z.)Squadron.
R.A.F. STATION.
BRADWELL BAY.

Flying Officer,
Intelligence Officer,
No 488 (N.Z.)Squadron.
R.A.F.STATION.
BRADWELL BAY.

3. This was the Combat Report of Pilot Officer Robinson and Flying Officer Clark, DFM, detailing their shooting down of a Messerschmitt 410 at Playden on 20th December 1943.

4. Flying Officer W.T.M. Clark, DFM, was the Navigator/Radar Operator in the Mosquito which claimed the Playden Messerschmitt.

5. The role of the policeman in war was often a difficult and dangerous one. Here, PC 169 William Watts gets ready for duty. Note his tin hat and the "black-out" cycle lamp. On 1st May 1944, this officer dealt with the crash of a P-51 Mustang at Brede in which Richard C. Hughes of the USAAF was unfortunately burnt to death.

7. 2nd. Lt. Bob Benton of the USAAF had a lucky escape at Iden Lock on 16th July 1944.

6. On 27th May 1944, a Spitfire crashed at Ashes Farm, Icklesham. Here are four 303 machine guns and one of the 20mm cannons recovered from the crash site in the 1970s.

8. Fg. Off. George Kosh was killed at Winchelsea on 1st July 1944, as he chased a V1 Flying Bomb in his fighter.

9. This is the aeroplane in which George Kosh died, Tempest JN765 of 3 Squadron, RAF.

10. On 23rd July 1944, two USAAF P-47 Thunderbolt fighters collided over Battle when flying in formation like this. Both pilots baled out and one P-47 crashed at Beauport Park, the other at Kent Street, Sedlescombe.

11. On 28th November 1944, a V2 Rocket exploded above Burwash, extensively damaging the elegant Southover Hall. Some buildings on the estate were wrecked, the Hall itself later converted to flats.

BEXHILL MUNICIPAL BOROUGH

The year 1943 opened with the tragedy of an attack in which Suffolk House, a Nursing Home in Brassey Road was bombed, killing three elderly residents and one of the staff. It proved to be a portent of things to come, for this year would see the lives of nine of Bexhill's civilian population claimed through air raid activity.

At the end of the month, on the 28th, raiders hit the Gasworks at Glyne Gap seriously injuring William Day and Bertram Niner. Both men were later to succumb to their injuries. There followed a lull until Sunday 23rd May when Focke Wulf 190 fighter bombers swept along the seafront at 1pm bombing and machine gunning as they went. They had just hit Hastings badly and now delivered a parting shot at Bexhill as they sped out to sea. Bombs falling in Westville Road killed Edith Few and Lily Smith, but two of the raiding force of aircraft were reported shot down into the sea.

On 30th June a Spitfire was wrecked in a forced landing at Sweet Willow Wood on the Ninfield Road following engine failure. Sgt. Pilot Ian Hastings of 501 Squadron escaped with injuries to his right eye but after local treatment was returned to his unit at Hawkinge.

Dramatic events unfolded along this part of the Sussex coast when, on 6th September, B-17 Flying Fortress aircraft of the USAAF came down in considerable numbers in the sea and just inland. The aircraft were returning from an attack on Stuttgart where bad weather and fighter attacks had caused mayhem with the raiding force. Damaged and short of fuel the returning bombers put down where they could, and one ditched in rough seas just off Bexhill seafront. Nineteen year old Lt. Cox and his crew were rescued by two local fishermen in rowing boats as the Fortress broke up and sank beneath the waves.

Another Spitfire, this time flown by a Belgian, Flt. Lt. Seydel, came down at Constables Farm, Bexhill, on 14th December and, although the aeroplane was damaged, Seydel was unharmed and returned to his unit at RAF Friston. On the night of 22nd/23rd December German bombs hit 5 Gloucester Avenue and seriously injured four year old Muriel Watson who died of her injuries at Bexhill Hospital later on the 23rd. This tragedy was the last civilian life lost in Bexhill through enemy action during the 1939-45 war.

The year was seen out by the ditching of a USAAF B-24 Liberator just offshore on 30th December when returning damaged from a raid on Ludwigshafen. Six of the crew were rescued, but the event was notable in that it saw one of the first successful ditchings in this type of aircraft which were notoriously difficult to put down on water.

For Bexhill there followed a lull in activity of some six months - but this could truly be called the calm before the storm! With the unleashing of the V1 Flying Bomb attacks on 13th June 1944, Bexhill found itself in the appropriately named "Bomb Alley". For around 80 days the missiles passed overhead, day and night. In one 24 hour period no fewer than 48 Flying Bombs were tracked over the town and in the overall duration of attacks at least seventeen of these deadly missiles fell in the Borough and several others were exploded in mid-air by fighters or anti aircraft guns. Incredibly, there were no civilian deaths as a result of these attacks although one soldier was killed. Damage, however, was considerable and numerous properties were either damaged or destroyed in the town.

Fighter patrols mounted to counter the V1 menace had a high success rate, although in combating "robot" weapons the cost to the RAF in aircrews was significant. Indeed, on 31st July, a Tempest and Spitfire, both intent on chasing the same flying bomb, failed to see each other and collided. The Spitfire crashed to earth at Sandhurst Lane, killing Fg. Off. "Paddy" Schade.

Exactly one month later, on 31st August, another "V1 related" RAF loss occurred in the district. This time a bomb laden Lancaster of 625 Squadron, outbound to attack V1 launch sites in France, experienced an out-of-control inner starboard engine. Over speeding and on fire the flames from the engine fanned to a white hot heat and threatened to burn through the wing spar, forcing the seven crew to bale out. Six were uninjured, but one broke an ankle on landing. Fortunately, the bomber crashed just short of Barnhorn and none of fifteen high explosive bombs detonated on impact. Had the burning and crewless bomber continued on its eastward track and crashed into Little Common or Bexhill the consequences could have been horrific. As it was, the only casualty on the ground was reported to be one "slightly injured" cow!

As the V1 attacks diminished and stopped when the Allies over-ran the launch sites in Northern France the sudden calm after such frantic activity made it seem that the war was well and truly over and the crash of a tiny Piper Cub at Charters Towers on 6th December must have seemed something of an anti-climax to the emergency services - now well used to dealing with almost every eventuality that war could bring!

In 1945 there were no incidents reported which were worthy of mention - save for the odd sea mine washed up by the tides on Bexhill's beaches. When it was all over the tally of civilian deaths in air raids stood at 21, with scores more injured and widespread damage and destruction. Genteel Bexhill-on-Sea had experienced a far from genteel five years of war.

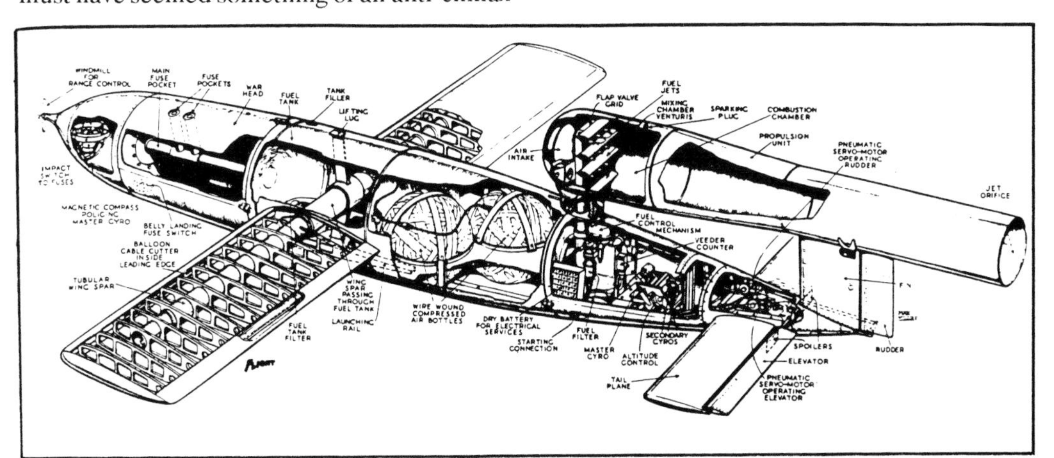

Officially, it was the Fiesler Fi 103 - otherwise known as Vergeltungswaffe 1, or V1. To the British it was simply the V1, Flying Bomb or Doodlebug. 374 of them fell in Battle Rural District.

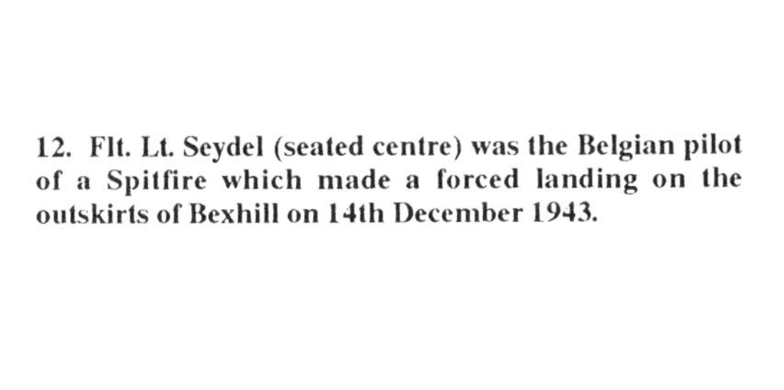

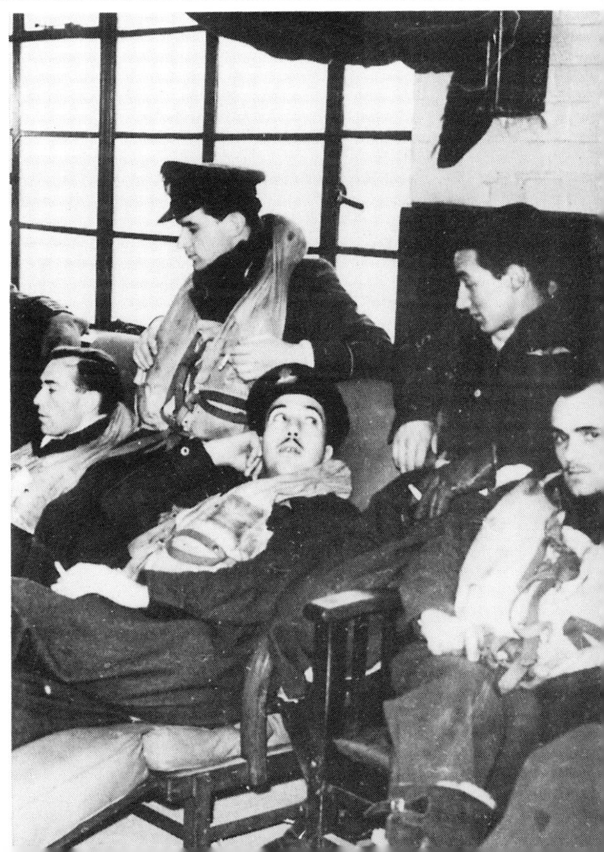

12. Flt. Lt. Seydel (seated centre) was the Belgian pilot of a Spitfire which made a forced landing on the outskirts of Bexhill on 14th December 1943.

BOGNOR REGIS URBAN DISTRICT

The first air attack of the period came on 5th February 1943, when there was widespread bomb damage at Albert Road, Bognor Pavilion, the Merchant Taylors Chapel and at various shops around the town centre. Two people were killed in Albert Road and a number of people were injured, some seriously.

Tragedy overtook Plt. Off. J. M. Cremer of 610 Squadron on 14th March when he stalled off a climbing turn in his Spitfire, crashed into the sea off Bognor and was killed outright. The next month, on 22nd, a similar fate befell Sgt. E. H. Fletcher of 197 Squadron when his Typhoon spun into the ground and crashed at Beatty Road, Bognor. Unfortunately, this episode had tragic consequences for the residents of Beatty Road; 56 year old Leonard Martlew being killed as he worked in his garden and a Miss Daisy Smith of Havelock Road sustaining burns and shock. The body of Sgt. Fletcher was later found in his smashed and burnt out Typhoon amidst the rubble and debris of wrecked houses.

The next aircraft incident involved a Mosquito which went into the sea 250 yards south of Strandway on 30th November with the loss of Fg. Off. A. W. Berry and Sgt. D. Walsh. Two unexploded 500lb bombs were later found on the beach and were rendered safe by an RAF Bomb Disposal Squad.

The sea continued to claim victims and on the 9th February 1944, an RAF Mustang of 170 Squadron went down off Bognor, followed on the 24th by a German Heinkel 177 bomber.

On 26th April it seems that Bognor had a lucky escape as a night raider dumped four bombs which exploded harmlessly in the sea off Bognor Pier. But for a matter of a few hundred yards the episode could have had a rather different outcome.

When D-Day dawned on 6th June the people of Bognor awoke to an amazing sight and sound as the air filled with hundreds of aircraft towing assault gliders - all heading for France. All passed overhead apparently without mishap, although records show that parachutes and stores were apparently dropped from one of the gliders just off Bognor. Presumably the glider got into some sort of difficulty and it is possible that it latter came down at sea because one of the Shoreham based High Speed Rescue Launches of the RAF's Marine Craft Unit reports the rescue of six soldiers from a ditched glider on this date.

At Rose Green on 7th June, farm workers had a lucky escape when a unidentified device exploded in a field of straw which was being burnt off. The blast caused a 6 ft crater and it was fortunate there were no casualties and no damage was caused.

The next day a Spitfire of 441 (RCAF) Squadron made a crash landing at Chessels Farm, Flansham, after its engine had failed on take-off. Flt. Lt. A. Johnstone was unhurt.

Independence Day 1944, saw a dramatic event at Felpham in when a B-17 Flying Fortress with two engines out of action and a third faltering put down in sugar beet field and overran into the gardens of houses in Downview Road. Lt. Mayo. R. Adams Jnr. had been lucky to get his crew home safely, and of the nine on board six were unhurt, two had slight wounds from shrapnel and a third dislocated his shoulder in the crash. The four engined bomber, named " Twentieth Century", had stopped just feet from the Downview Road houses, in one of which Miss Ethel Cheney stood riveted to the spot by her kitchen sink as the bomber thundered towards her. When it stopped the crew all piled out onto her lawn, whooping with relief and delight. Drying her hands, Miss Cheney walked down the garden towards the American fliers and enquired of them " Would you like tea?".

For most places in Sussex west of Seaford there was remarkably little Flying Bomb activity once the V1 campaign began. At Bognor, however, a stray specimen dropped between Shelley Road and Tennyson Road on 27th August and exploded causing considerable devastation. In total there were 65 people injured and some 550 houses were damaged.

Bognor's V1 proved to be the last of its 85 wartime "incidents" which had claimed the lives of 22 civilians in the Borough. On 8th May 1945, its relieved inhabitants celebrated VE Day with some considerable gusto.

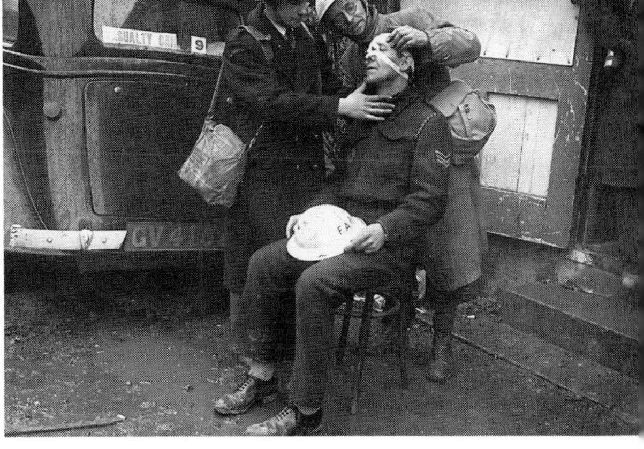

13. An ARP worker, injured in the aftermath of the 5th February raid on Bognor, receives First Aid.

14. The stalwart band of Bognor's Air Raid Wardens in 1943 (Can fans of "Dad's Army " spot a Mr. Hodges in there somewhere?)

15. This was the tragic scene at Beatty Road, Bognor, on 22nd April 1943, after the crash of an RAF Typhoon. Firemen and other rescuers douse the flames and search for bodies.

16. Men of the Bognor Regis Home Guard carry out a mock attack on the Town Hall during 1943. Note that the entrance has been bricked-up and turned into a public air raid shelter. The "S" sign says Shelter Here and indicates a capacity of 22 persons.

17. The " Twentieth Century " comes to Downview Road! This was the scene at the end of Miss Cheney's garden on Independence Day 1944.

18. Re-cycling is nothing new! Here, Bognor's Civil Defence workers lend a hand with wartime paper salvage.

19. Street parties were held all across England to celebrate VE Day on 8th May 1945. Here, the children of Lyon Street enjoy the happy event.

BRIGHTON COUNTY BOROUGH

Brighton's first major raid of 1943 took place on 25th March when Focke Wulf 190's raided the town and scattered bombs over a wide area. Particularly badly hit were Gloucester Place, Grosvenor Street, Circus Street and Sussex Street where a total of eighteen people were killed, including three young children at the Circus Street Chest Clinic.

On 24th April, shortly after midnight, a Mosquito crashed outside the town at Falmer, on Housedean Farm by the Lewes Road and burnt out. So badly burned and smashed was the wreckage that the Police were unable to identify either of the two occupants, only a burnt cheque book stub providing any clues. Eventually it was established that the two occupants were Sqn. Ldr. Ian Bocock and Sgt. Robert Brown of 605 Squadron.

The fighter-bombers were back again on 25th May when a force of up to 25 Focke Wulf 190's struck the town at around mid-day, killing 24 people and seriously injuring 51. During this raid there was some particularly serious and spectacular damage. One bomb fell in Argyle Road, bounced over houses and exploded against the railway viaduct bringing down one entire span whilst leaving the railway track suspended in mid-air. Another bomb hit the steps at Lovers Walk and ricocheted into the Pullman Car Works where it did considerable damage, whilst a further bomb wrecked two empty trains standing close to the main line and threw debris from smashed rolling stock high over the chalk cutting into the gardens of bomb-damaged houses along Stanford Road. The Brighton Running Sheds were also set ablaze and severely damaged. There were other attacks in 1943 - particularly during August and October - though none were as serious as the big raid of 25th May.

Also in May, on the 7th, Sgt. Pilot J. Hill of 197 Squadron lost control of his Typhoon and spun into the ground at Graham Avenue, losing his life as a result.

Another Typhoon, this time of 274 Squadron, crash landed on Downland to the east of Brighton on 2nd February 1944, although Plt. Off. J. Boyer escaped unharmed. February also saw the return of German bombers on 23rd, killing and injuring a number of people at Bennett Road. It proved to be the last attack on Brighton which resulted in serious loss of life, although the very last raid on Brighton was not until 22nd March 1944.

Earlier, on 8th February, a homecoming B-17 Flying Fortress of the 384th Bomb Group made a miraculous landing in fields alongside the London Road at Patcham. Two of the ten crew on board had been injured and the aeroplane, named " Winsome Win II ", was damaged. However, the Fortress was repaired on site and flown out some days later after hedges had been removed, ditches filled in and overhead lines taken down.

Equally if not more dramatic was the shooting down of a Messerschmitt 410 which crashed at night on 19th April into St. Nicholas Churchyard, Dyke Road. Hit by cannon and machine-gun fire from a Mosquito flown by Wg. Cdr. E. D. Crew, DFC, and W/O W. R. Croysdill the stricken bomber dived into the tombstones and churchyard wall, blasting a large crater and scattering debris around the churchyard and along Dyke Road. The pilot, Oblt Richard Pahl, did not escape from his aeroplane and his body was found hanging in nearby trees. Fortunately, bombs on board the Messerchmitt failed to explode and were found in the wreckage, but of the gunner, Fw. Wilhelm Schubert, no trace could at first be found. Eventually, his body was washed ashore and buried at Friston, he having baled out over the sea and drowned. Pahl, meanwhile, was buried in Brighton's Bear Road Cemetery where his well tended grave may still be seen.

On 26th November 1944, a Hudson aircraft was returning from Europe with a VIP passenger and with four Typhoon's as escort when one of the escorting fighters hit the West Pier and crashed onto the beach. Flt. Lt. J. Brown received head injuries and the Typhoon's port wing was badly damaged in what was to be the last wartime air crash in the Borough.

When it came time to reckon up the cost on VE-Day it was found that 198 civilians had been killed and 988 injured in a total of 56 air raids which had also destroyed over 200 houses and damaged at least 11,392 other properties. One can imagine the relief, therefore, after Brighton's air raid siren had sounded the " all clear" for the 1,058th and last time!

20. The Pullman Car Workshop at Brighton and associated rolling stock were wrecked in another fighter-bomber attack on 25th May 1943.

21. This was the spectacular damage to the Brighton railway viaduct on 25th May 1943. Also see pictures 15 and 16 in *Brighton to Eastbourne (Middleton Press)*.

22. Work gets under way to urgently repair the damage with the double track still suspended precariously in mid air!

23. Although the threat of invasion had receded or passed, the Home Guard continued in being until November 1944. This " Secret " Memo sets out the disposition of the 10th (Sussex) East Brighton Home Guard and details its Officers, HQ's and Battle Stations.

MUCH OF THIS INFORMATION IS
SEE THAT IT REMAINS SO **SECRET**

GENERAL KNOWLEDGE: "B" COMPANY

LOCATION LISTS: 10th (SX) EAST BRIGHTON H.G.

BATTALION HEADQUARTERS:

C.O.: LT.-COL. FILKINS, M.C. 2 I/C: MAJOR COXHEAD, M.C.
Adjt.: CAPT. CLAYTON, M.C. Q.M.: CAPT. CRISTEN. R.Q.M.S. THOMPSON.
M.O.: MAJOR WALKER. L.O.: CAPT. BASTOCK.
H.Q. Platoon Commander: LIEUT. BALLARD. 2 I/C: 2nd LIEUT. ORCHARD.
I.O.: LIEUT. MacLARNON. Tpt.O.: LIEUT. BUDD-BUDD. Sigs. O.: LIEUT. MOODY.
Gas and Amm. O.: 2nd LIEUT. BARNWELL. Musketry O.: LIEUT. BROWN.
M.G. O.: LIEUT. CUNNINGHAM. R.S.M. GASTON. P.S.I.: S.M. VINALL.
Garrison Comd.: LT.-COL. KERR (Devonian Court). Training Officer: MAJOR MORRISON.

BATT. HEADQUARTERS: 22, SUSSEX SQUARE.
Tel. Brighton 1105. Tel. (Sigs.) Brighton 5280.

"A" COMPANY

Adm.: FLINT HOUSE, ROTTINGDEAN Tel. Rottingdean 9124.
Battle Station: OVINGDEAN GRANGE, ROTTINGDEAN.
Tel. Rottingdean 9143.
O.C.: MAJOR BRITTEN. 2 I/C: (Acting) Lt. SARGEANT. Platoon Nos. 1, 2, 3 and 4.

"B" COMPANY

Coy. H.Q.: "SUNNYSIDE," UPPER LEWES ROAD, BRIGHTON.
Tel. Brighton 1664.
Battle Station H.Q.: GRANDSTAND, RACEHILL.
O.C.: MAJOR WALKER. 2 I/C: CAPTAIN VIRGO.
I.Sjt.: Sjt. OSBORNE. C.S.M. HEMMINGS. C.Q.M.S. BROOKS.

5 PLATOON—Com.: LT. DIVALL. 2 I/C: 2nd LT. HOPWOOD. Pl. Sjt.: Sjt. RAPSON.
Battle Station: WRIGHT'S FARM.

6 PLATOON—Com.: LT. BRISTOW. 2 I/C: 2nd LT. BRINGEMAN. Pl. Sjt.: Sjt. GAWEN.
Battle Station: 2, CHAPEL TERRACE.

7 PLATOON—Com. (Acting): LT. EALES. 2 I/C (Acting): Sjt. GUNN, W. S. Pl. Sjt. ——
Battle Station: GRANDSTAND, RACEHILL.

8 PLATOON—Com.: LT. WRATTEN. 2 I/C: 2nd LT. HAMPTON. Pl. Sjt.: Sjt. MARTIN.
Battle Station: GRANDSTAND, RACEHILL.

9 PLATOON—Com.: LT. STILL. 2 I/C: 2nd LT. RUSSELL. Pl. Sjt.: Sjt. BEHR.
Battle Station: 359 COASTAL BATTERY, ROYAL ARTILLERY, CHICHESTER TERRACE.

"D" COMPANY

Company and Battle Station H.Q.:
DRILL HALL, GLOUCESTER ROAD. Tel.: Brighton 3653.
O.C.: MAJOR THOMERSON. 2 I/C: CAPT. PRATT. Platoon Nos. 13, 14, 15 and 16.

"F" COMPANY

Company and Battle Station H.Q.:
QUEEN SQUARE, BRIGHTON. Tel. Brighton 2586.
O.C.: MAJOR ATFIELD. 2 I/C: CAPT. ALBUTT. Platoon Nos. 21, 22, 23 and 24.

24. Mangled wreckage from a Messerschmitt 410 is strewn amongst the tombstones of St. Nicholas Churchyard, Brighton, on 19th April 1944.

25. Another view of the St. Nicholas Churchyard crash.

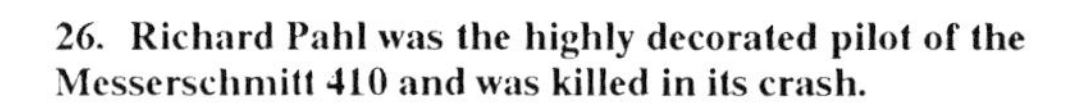

26. Richard Pahl was the highly decorated pilot of the Messerschmitt 410 and was killed in its crash.

27. High and dry this battered Typhoon sits on Brighton Beach following a collision with the West Pier.

BURGESS HILL URBAN DISTRICT

This tiny district escaped any serious consequences of enemy action right from 1940 to the end of 1942. Indeed, the period covered by this book 1943 to 1945, saw the fortunes of Burgess Hill hold good until the end of hostilities. Even during the Flying Bomb period these missiles went over but not on Burgess Hill! All the same, it was during that particular period, on 12th July 1944, that the human tragedy of war touched the district.

In a practice dogfight at 15,000 ft above the town two Spitfires wheeled and dived as each chased the other around the sky. Suddenly, something went wrong and one of the aeroplanes went into a vertical dive from 8,000 ft from which it did not pull out. Roaring at full-throttle the Spitfire smashed into the ground at Greenlands Field, Keymer Road, and blew to pieces. On the ground, damage was confined to several trees and to a number of cows which were grazing the field at the time. Two houses, "Parklands" and "Paddocks", were also slightly damaged but it was only when Inspector Brown of the Haywards Heath Police Division examined the wreckage that it became clear the pilot had not escaped. Contrary to both local legend and previously published sources the pilot was not Polish. Instead, he was Fg. Off. A. A. Ghislain Patiny, a Belgian, serving with 349 Squadron, RAF. No definite cause for the crash could ever be established, but it was considered likely that Patiny had become air sick and disorientated during violent manoeuvers and that he subsequently lost control of the aeroplane.

It was with a sigh of relief, no doubt, that Burgess Hill's Civil Defence volunteers hung up their overalls and tin-hats at the wars end. It could so easily have been a different story and when they looked at surrounding districts which had suffered so badly they could only reflect on how lucky they had been.

CHAILEY RURAL DISTRICT

Dornier 217 aircraft had ranged freely across the county on 10th February 1943, and bombed Chichester, Midhurst and Hailsham. These attacks were not without cost to the Luftwaffe, though, and two of the Dorniers were brought down in the county. At Saltdean one of the raiders , hit by anti-aircraft fire, fell in a field close to the bungalows and houses in Holmbush Avenue. None of the four crew survived when the aircraft disintegrated and burnt out.

At Swanborough Farm, Iford, on 16th August a Polish pilot, Sgt Waclaw Korwel, crash landed his battle damaged Spitfire which had been riddled with machine gun and cannon fire. One bullet had gone through the cockpit door, passed through Korwel's left hand and smashed the instrument panel. Despite his wounds, and the damage to the aeroplane, Korwel managed to get his Spitfire down safely in a field of standing corn.

Returning from a raid on Duren a B-17 Flying Fortress of the 96th Bomb Group was abandoned by its crew and crashed south of Furlongs Farm, Beddingham, on 20th October. The scattered wreckage provided a rich harvest of .50 calibre cannon shells and broken perspex for the local schoolboy population who would cycle for miles to reach such rich pickings of trophies!

As the New Year opened, so began the Luftwaffe's Operation Steinbock - or The Little Blitz as it became known to the British. A major effort by the German bomber force saw renewed night attacks on London on 21st January. However, the raids were something of a failure and saw flare paths set down across the whole of Chailey Rural District which was then heavily bombed with incendiary and high explosive devices. There was little damage and no casualties - although it had been a rather alarming night. Nevertheless, an apparent navigational error had spared London at least some of the death and destruction intended for it that night.

Night raiders again bombed the area on 23rd February - this time littering incendiary bombs across Plumpton. There were some remarkable escapes in this raid when bombs smashed through the roof of several Council houses. In one, a Mrs. Arnold was struck on the head by an incendiary bomb as she lay in bed with her children. She was burnt, but managed to get her children to safety before receiving treatment. Nearby, 12 year old Gerald Matthews was in bed with his four year old brother, Robin, when an incendiary fell on the bed between them setting light to the covers. The older boy and his mother smothered the flames and nobody was hurt. At the Sun Inn, 80 year old Mr. Downey was trapped in his burning bedroom by an incendiary bomb which had jammed shut the door. The door was broken down by his son, Captain L.A. Downey, and nobody seemed any the worse for the experience! This remarkable good fortune stayed with Chailey Rural District and, there were no civilian fatalities in the area during the period covered by this book.

On the airfield at Plumpton a B-17 Flying Fortress exploded on 3rd August, damaging five houses and buildings at Parsonage Farm. Fortunately, there were no civilian casualties.

The year drew towards a close with a tragic episode on the 19th November involving another American aircraft, this time a DC-3 Dakota which crashed near Newmarket Plantation above Falmer. Witnesses saw the aeroplane flying very low from west to east and then vanish behind a ridge followed by a long sheet of flame and an explosion. All of the occupants were American servicemen and although there were several survivors, 23 were killed or died later in hospital.

When the tally was taken on VE Day there had been 381 bombs on the district, and between 12,000 and 14,000 incendiaries. 16 Flying bombs had fallen in the area, which was on the western fringe of the main "shooting alley" for these weapons. Fortunately, there were no Flying Bomb related fatalities although the Vicar of Firle, Revd. A.G. Gregor, was injured by one. Fortunately, there were only three civilian fatalities in the District and these all occurred in 1940 and 1941. It had been a frightening and dangerous five years, but it could easily have been so much worse.

28. On 10th February 1943, a Dornier 217 was shot down by anti-aircraft fire at Saltdean. Smashed up wreckage was all that remained.

29. One of the main wheels from the Saltdean Dornier 217.

30. Disaster struck a USAAF DC-3 Dakota troop transport which crashed into the Downs Newmarket Plantation on 19th November 1944. Twenty three of those on board perished.

CHANCTONBURY RURAL DISTRICT

In common with Chailey, Chanctonbury R.D. only suffered three civilian fatalities in the duration of the war. One of these, 73 year old Mary Richardson, died when her home at 41, Church Street, Steyning, was hit on 18th February 1943. She was the last civilian killed in the district, although the air war continued with unabated ferocity.

At Amberley, on 21st September, an RAF Mustang dived into a meadow near the railway station during a training flight killing Pilot Officer J. Elms of 4 Squadron. The wreckage buried itself on impact and then burnt fiercely, leaving those trying to recover the body of Elms with a grisly and unenviable task.

A similar task presented itself to the same salvage gang on 26th April 1944, when two Spitfires collided over Washington. One of them, flown by Wing Commander Roy Marples, dived into the ground at Lower Chancton Farm killing the Wing Commander outright. When rescuers arrived at the scene they found the plane had vanished into the soft clay. Burning petrol on the surface was extinguished by Storrington NFS, after which it was found that only small parts of the Spitfire protruded from a crater filled with water and petrol. Digging operations finally retrieved the body of the 24 year old officer, although much of the aircraft remained buried until it was salvaged in 1974. The other Spitfire which collided with Marples' aeroplane was less critically damaged and the pilot survived a crash-landing at Wappingthorn Farm, Steyning.

On the 25th June, during the early hours, the two crew of a 418 Squadron Mosquito were forced to abandon their machine leaving it to crash into a ditch at Red Barn, Upper Beeding. When dawn broke little was left on the surface to show that a twin engined aeroplane had crashed here and most of the wreckage had simply vanished into the soft clay.

A harrowing incident was dealt with by Police and emergency services during the late afternoon of 6th February 1945, when a B-17 Flying Fortress crashed 500 yards South-East of Truleigh Hill and was completely wrecked. All ten crewmen were killed on impact, and such was the ferocity of the crash that Police Officers were only able to identify four of the smashed bodies. Although the District had escaped relatively lightly in terms of civilian casualties the service death toll through aerial activity had been high - Germans, Poles, Frenchmen, Canadians, Australians, Englishmen and Americans had all lost their lives or been injured through aerial combat and flying mishaps over the Chanctonbury area.

31. This tiny snap is the only photographic record of the smashed-up B-17 Flying Fortress at Truleigh Hill on 6th February 1945. The letter "W" and aircraft number can be distinguished.

32. These were the two 20mm cannons recovered in 1974 from the crashed Spitfire at Washington. As "prohibited weapons" they were surrendered to the Police annd later destroyed.

33. This was Mosquito HJ719 of 418 Squadron, abandoned by its crew after engine failure on an operational flight on 25th June 1944. The aeroplane crashed at Red Barn, Beeding.

CHICHESTER MUNICIPAL BOROUGH

One of the worst air aid incidents in the city took place on 10th February 1943. In a harrowing attack high explosive bombs were scattered across the city causing widespread casualties and damage to property. Badly hit were Chapel Street, North Street and St. Martins Street and when the death toll was finally taken at least seventeen civilians had lost their lives. To even the score a little, though, a Dornier 217 was engaged by anti-aircraft fire over Tangmere and brought down at Lagness (See Chichester Rural District for this date).

It was not until 26th April 1944, at seven minutes past midnight, that bombs again caused widespread havoc in the city. This time, four 500kg bombs fell; one in Armdale Road, one at St. James School and two at Bridge Road. Casualties totalled 37, of whom 7 were killed, 17 seriously injured and 13 slightly injured. These figures, quoted in the local Police reports, conflict with Home Office returns which show five fatalities.

Property too was damaged on a massive scale, 468 dwelling houses being affected to a greater or lesser degree by blast.

Still reeling from this attack the city was to suffer another blow on llth May when a USAAF B-24 Liberator bomber crashed into The Hornet. Returning from a raid over Europe where the bomber had been hit and set on fire the crew baled out on crossing the coast and the pilot then put his aircraft on course to crash into the sea. Unfortunately, the crewless plane turned back and headed for the centre of Chichester where it crashed. Wreckage was strewn across the Whyke Lane and Green Lane area, damaging a garage, St. John's School, allotments, Longs Timber Yard and setting fire to the City Electric Laundry. At the laundry fifty women and girls were working and the building, doused in aviation fuel, was set alight and burning fiercely within minutes. Sadly, fourteen year old Ellen Grainger was killed outright in the laundry and fifty nine year old Elizabeth Tess succumbed to her injuries three days later. Adding to the scene of carnage, two 1,000 lb bombs exploded in the flaming wreckage injuring Anne Humphreys and Special Constable Leonard Price, both of whom died later from their injuries. Twenty seven other persons were injured, fourteen of them seriously, and a staggering total of 704 houses were damaged. Of the crew, all ten landed safely by parachute although two were detained in hospital - the pilot, Lt. Duncan, was deeply shocked by the horrors his stricken Liberator has inflicted upon the City, despite heroic efforts to save his crew and to send his unmanned charge back out to sea. Such were the fortunes of war.

An end to this terrible period seemed finally in sight when, on 6th June, the whole of Southern England awoke to the roar of an awesome outgoing armada of aircraft bound for Normandy. On the ground, movements of troops and vehicles were seen on an unprecedented scale - D-Day had dawned. The moment of hope, though, was tempered by the subsequent influx of casualties by the hundred into the Royal West Sussex Hospital, St. Richards Hospital and Summersdale Emergency Hospital. Whole wards had been cleared, and teams of nurses and doctors stood by to receive the wounded, delivered by fleets of ambulances which trundled constantly through the City. To the citizens it was a salutary reminder that final victory, though now in sight, would not be achieved without a further awful price in human suffering.

When VE Day finally came, Chichester could draw comfort from the fact that despite some terrible air raids it had never experienced the round-the-clock bombing suffered by many British cities during the Blitz. It had also escaped largely unscathed from the curse of fighter bomber hit and run attacks, and its precious Cathedral had never been targeted during the German "Baedecker" raids against sites of cultural importance. Though battle scarred and war weary the City had much to be thankful for.

34. Bomb damage in Chichester after the raid of 10th February 1943. Perhaps this was Reeve's Garage in North Street where sixteen year old Norman Lawrence was killed?.

35. Tragedy struck Chichester on 11th May 1944, when a B-24 Liberator like one of these shown here crashed into the city. Four civilians were killed in this terrible tragedy and there was widespread damage.

CHICHESTER RURAL DISTRICT

Covering the largest geographical area of all the Rural Districts in the county, and containing the active aerodromes of Ford, Tangmere, and Thorney Island and a dozen or so smaller or Advanced Landing Grounds, it was inevitable that Chichester would see the greatest number of aircraft losses by far.

The first loss was an RAF B-24 Liberator of 86 Squadron (No.LV346) which crashed into Thorney Channel on 12th January 1943, killing some of the crew. This, however, was not the first aeroplane which had come down in the mud of Thorney Channel - nor would it be the last!

Notable for the widespread bombing attacks across the county, 10th February also saw the loss on one of the raiders - a Dornier 217 shot down by ground defences at Tangmere to crash near the Royal Oak, Lagness, with all four crew killed. (In 1944 a Bognor Regis youth was badly injured by a German cannon shell he found at this crash site and which exploded as he polished it)

Two other young lads, ATC Cadets, had a lucky escape on 24th April when the Thorney Island based Hampden in which they were being given an air-experience flight collided with a Spitfire in mid-air and crashed at Headhone Farm, Lidsey, catching fire as it struck a pole in the field. The two boys were both thrown out of the wreckage, but Edmund Gleaves was seriously injured and Arthur Bint suffered a badly cut nose and lip. Two farm workers, Leslie Ayling and John Wickham, rushed to the burning plane and dragged the crew clear. Unfortunately, the pilot, Flt. Sgt. J. C. Donald, died later in hospital.

The story of the Typhoon which crashed into Pagham Harbour on 19th June is a fascinating though sad one. The story revolves around its pilot, P/O Kenneth Clift. Taking off from his Selsey base on 19th June, Clift was designated to conduct an air test of Typhoon DN293. Shortly after becoming airborne he spotted a Mosquito transitting the area and engaged it in unauthorised low-level mock combat. During this "sport" something went horribly wrong and Clift's Typhoon was seen to spiral into the harbour after conducting a loop. Clift was killed instantly, and the young pilot was later buried at Chichester. However, his gravestone reveals an intriguing mystery and shows his real identity to be Thomas Barker, an Australian, who had served in the RNZAF as Kenneth Clift. Why this subterfuge? Research in 1983 revealed that Barker had "borrowed" the identity of his friend, Ken Clift, and fled to New Zealand in 1937 after matrimonial problems and a "....little local difficulty" with the tax-man! Joining up when the war started he trained, served and died as Kenneth Clift - this story being revealed by the real Ken Clift who survived his friend with the "nomme-de-geurre" he lent him.

The story of Ken Clift's Typhoon did not end until 1984 when the engine and much of the wreckage was recovered by the Tangmere Aviation Museum with the help of a USAF heavy lift helicopter. The engine and propeller may be seen on display at the Tangmere Museum.

On the night of 19th/20th November there was tragedy at Tangmere when a 10 Squadron Halifax, returning from a raid on Leverkusen crashed into a hanger and caught fire. All of the Halifax crew were killed, and seven fighter aircraft in the hanger were destroyed by fire.

An extraordinary episode was witnessed at breakfast time at Ford aerodrome on 10th September when a Messerschmitt 108 communications aircraft was seen approaching the 'drome firing signal flares. Following was a Mosquito fighter, which, unsure of the German's intent, opened fire on the Messerschmitt panicking the pilot into a crash landing. It was with some surprise that the authorities discovered the two occupants had suitcases full of clothes and personal belongings and that they had stolen the aeroplane from Chateaudun, France, intending to defect. Unfortunately, one of the two men, Uffz. Jonni Suppinger, died later in Ford's Sick Quarters at Tortington Hall. The other occupant, Uffz. Victor Pacher, was injured.

Throughout the remainder of 1943 there were many more aircraft losses around Chichester. One of the last incidents being the sad loss of two Special Duties Lysander aircraft of 161 Squadron on 16th December, returning to Tangmere from France where they had picked up important agents and members of the French Resistance. Returning home they found the South Coast blanketed in fog and one aeroplane crashed at Ford, another at Drayton Railway Crossing attempting to land at Tangmere. At Ford, Sqn.Ldr.Stephen Hankey was killed together with Lt. Albert Berthaud of the Free French Forces. Another occupant of this Lysander was injured and at Drayton Fg. Off. McBride (from Port of Spain, Trinidad) was killed and Stab. Major (French Navy) Jacques Tayar was badly injured, dying later in the Royal West Sussex Hospital. Another of his passengers survived. This was a disaster for the Intelligence Services and was shrouded in the greatest of secrecy with a terse Police report on the episode stating "All messages passed in connection with this incident to be cancelled. This has been done and no report submitted on Daily Summary" Such was the secrecy that even the Registration of Death for each man was entered by different and clearly fictitious RAF Officers!!

The next day Fg. Off. Edmund O'Callaghan of Fermoy, Co. Cork died when his Typhoon crashed at Bow Hill, Chilgrove, in bad visibility. Poor weather conditions frequently caused wartime aircraft losses, and many crashes occurred in this District for that reason. As will be seen, there were many more.

The following year was no less eventful in terms of aircraft losses and began with the forced-landing of a Spitfire out of fuel at Climping Farm Ford, on 5th January 1944. As the tally of aircraft down in the district increased it was surely inevitable that civilians on the ground would be killed as a consequence. This was the case on 30th January at Bilsham Corner, Yapton, when Mosquito HX916 flew into the ground in fog and broke up killing Fg. Off. J. Hyndman and W/O G. Matthews of 487 Squadron and two civilians, George Rogers, 82 and little Mary Ifould , aged 9.

On the 8th February, a Wellington of 180 Operational Training Unit was engaged on a night exercise with a Mosquito of 85 Squadron when the Mosquito accidentally rammed the Wellington from astern, severing the tail. The bomber plunged to earth at Wakefords Farm, Chidham, as the Mosquito went down out of control to crash just across the border into Hampshire. All the crew of the Wellington perished, as did the pilot of the Mosquito and his navigator. The Mosquito pilot was Arthur Woods, a pre-war film director of some repute who, had he survived, would doubtless have become a household name in the post-war cinema world.

Flying accidents continued at an alarming pace and as will be seen from the lists at the end of the book; hardly a week was to pass before yet another RAF or Allied aircraft came to grief in Sussex.

On 13th February a Lancaster of 617 ("Dambuster") Squadron came down on the top of Waltham Down, Upwaltham. Having returned from a raid against the Antheor Viaduct, S. France, the squadron's aircraft landed at 5am on their forward operating base of RAF Ford which they had used for this mission. At 8.20am, five minutes after leaving Ford, this aeroplane hit trees on top of the hill whilst returning to its home base of Woodhall Spa. The cause of the accident was put down to pilot error as he had been aware of low cloud conditions and should have been wary of the high ground to the North of Ford. Upon impact the Lancaster was badly broken up and caught fire - ammunition and flares going off in the burning wreckage. Six of the crew and one passenger, Sqn. Ldr. T. Lloyd, DSO, were killed instantly but the pilot, Sqn. Ldr. William Suggit, DFC, was rescued from the wreckage by Philip Chapman and Frederick Denyer of Upwaltham - without any thought for their own safety or the fact that bombs may be on board. Mr. H. Privett, Mr. G. Scutt and Ldg, Seaman R. J. Boyd, DSM, all assisted in searching for survivors and dragging the bodies clear. Sqn. Ldr. Suggitt died later that day in St. Richards Hospital, Chichester. The occupants of the Lancaster were all members of 617 Squadron and some of them were veterans of the famous Dams Raid. Lloyd, the passenger, was the Squadron Intelligence Officer and was being given a lift back to base.

At Walberton, on the night of 24th/25th March there was a welcome respite for the locals from the seemingly endless numbers of Allied aircraft falling in the area as a Junkers 88 fell to the guns of Wg. Cdr. Hampshire, DSO, and Fg. Off. Condon in their 456 Squadron Mosquito. The bomber broke up in the air and only one of the crew survived. One of the others was found, still alive, but with horrific injuries, having been buried in the ground up to his knees when his parachute failed to function properly.

On 10th March W/O Wakeman of the U.S. Army, based at Westgate House, was killed as he tampered with an explosive incendiary bomb at Stamner. Another American soldier was injured and taken to the Royal West Sussex Hospital in an episode which demonstrated the lethal nature of these bombs which were often collected as souvenirs.

In April, on the 9th of the month, there was a return to the familiar routine of an aircraft loss through accidental causes. This time a Thorney Island based Albacore of 415 Sqn. spun into the ground and burnt at Brinkmans Nurseries, Bosham, killing all four crew. The pilot had ignored his orders and carried out practice dogfighting at 600 ft when the minimum safe height had been given as 3,000 ft. Out of control, the pilot had no time to recover the Albacore from its spiral dive to earth.

On 23rd May 1944 there was tragedy at RAF Ford when a returning B-17 Fortress crashed into the bomb dump, caught fire and exploded. As D-Day loomed so the price of intensified aerial activity increased correspondingly.

Much has been written elsewhere about the part this region played in the D-Day operations, so will not be repeated here save to say that the scale of activities during and after the operation was truly awesome. Losses through accident or combat causes were high and on 9th June, three days after the Invasion, a Spitfire which was being brought in to replace one of these losses crashed at Marsh Farm Binsted, killing the Ferry Pool Pilot, Warrant Officer Rasmussen.

When it came, the V1 Campaign almost passed the District by - most of these weapons fell in the east of the county, there being comparatively few Flying Bomb incidents west of Cuckmere Haven. Flying Bombs which did fall in the area, however, included one at Sand Pit Wood, Park Farm, Eartham on 16th June causing slight damage to buildings and blast damage to a tree plantation. There were no casualties. Another example was at Lavant, on 25th June, 60 yards from Yarbrook Cottages. This was shot down by anti-aircraft fire and damaged six buildings and injured one person. At Madehurst, on 12th July, another V1 fell about 200 yards from Madehurst Church causing extensive damage to the church and rectory and killing one cow in a nearby field.

There continued a long catalogue of aircraft losses - all Allied - throughout the remainder of 1944. This trend continued on into 1945, with one particularly tragic episode at Thorney Island on 10th February. A Lancaster of 1667 Heavy Conversion Unit was engaged on a cross-country training flight when it entered cumulo-nimbus cloud and the pilot lost control. It was considered this was due to icing. The aeroplane then broke up in the air and fell earthwards on fire. There were no survivors from the seven man crew who were all still in the aircraft when it dived into the creek on the east side of Thorney Island and disappeared. Only five bodies could be located, and no trace of Flt. Off. Harold King or Sgt. Colin Woodhead was ever found. It was assumed they were buried deeply with the wreckage and an RAF Chaplain later held a prayer service over the spot. Officially, both men are still listed "Missing - No Known Grave". There can be no doubt, however, that the grave of Harold King and Colin Woodhead lies in the mud of Thorney Channel between Prinstead and Nutbourne.

Despite intense aerial activity there had been no civilian loss of life due to enemy action in the period 1943 - 45, although two civilians were killed by a crashing RAF aircraft. Nevertheless, the area had experienced war at first hand on an almost unprecedented scale.

Everyday life for almost everyone had been caught up in the efforts and events of war to the extent that when VE-Day came it was not only a joyous relief but also something of an anticlimax. For those who had lived through it, life would never be quite the same again.

36. This is Typhoon DN293 at RAF Selsey during 1943, just prior to its demise when it crashed into Pagham Harbour on 19th June 1943, killing its pilot.

37. Pilot of DN293 was Australian Pilot Officer Tom Barker, who served as Kenneth Clift of the Royal New Zealand Air Force!

38. The engine and propeller of Ken Clifts Typhoon are lifted out of Pagham Harbour by a USAF CH-53 helicopter in 1984.

39. Returning from a raid on Leverkusen on 19th November 1943, Stirling BK762 crashed on landing at Ford. Flt.Lt. Guthrie, Fg. Off. Perry and Flt. Sgt. Duroe pose by their belly-landed bomber.

40. Pilots and groundcrew with one of the "secret" Lysanders of 161 (Special Duties) Sqn. at Tangmere in 1943. These aeroplanes were used to fly agents in and out of occupied Europe under cover of darkness.

41. Tangmere Cottage was the operational H.Q. for 161 Squadron's highly secret work. Today it is a private residence.

42. Squadron Leader Stephen Alers Hankey was pilot of a 161 Squadron Lysander and was killed trying to land in thick fog at RAF Ford when returning from France with Resistance workers and SOE agents. He is buried at Crowhurst in East Sussex.

43. The burnt remains of a Fairey Albacore which crashed at Brinkmans Nurseries, Bosham, on 9th April 1944.

46. On the night of 24th/25th March 1944 Wg. Co Keith Hampshire and Fg. Off. Tom Condon of 45 (RAAF) Sqn. shot down a Junkers 88 over the distric Here they examine the smashed up wreck at Walberto

47. A Chaplain conducts an open air service fo Canadians near Selsey on the eve of D-Day, 5th Jun 1944. Tented encampments like this we commonplace in Sussex during the Spring and ear Summer of 1944. On 6th June they were sudden empty.

48. Their Majesties King George V1 and Quee Elizabeth at RAF Tangmere on 14th July 1944, for a fie investiture. They are seated outside the Officers Me which has since been demolished.

44. A huge column of smoke and flame rises from the bomb dump at RAF Ford after a crippled B-17 Flying Fortress had crashed into it on 23rd May, 1944.

45. In the run-up to D-Day, General Eisenhower the Supreme Allied Commander, took lunch with senior air officers in the Mess at RAF Tangmere. He is seen here seated extreme left.

20

49. NAAFI girls inspect the cockpit of a Spitfire MK.IX of 303 (Polish) Squadron at RAF Westhampnett in December 1944. The large Type T2 hangar still exists on what is now known as Goodwood Aerodrome.

50. When Lancaster W4890 plunged into Thorney Channel on 10th February, 1945, all seven crew members lost their lives. Amongst them was Bomb Aimer P/O Harold King, seen here with his fiancee shortly before his death on active service. No trace of Harold's body was ever found.

51. The Fighter Experimental Flight was one of the many RAF units stationed at Ford. This is their 1944 "scoreboard".

FIGHTER EXPERIMENTAL FLIGHT
(RANGER.)
VICTORIES

FORMED OCT. 27TH 1944 — OPERATIONAL 1ST JAN.- 8TH MAY 1945

AIRCREWS	NO. OF SORTIES	A/C DESTROYED	A/C PROBABLY DESTROYED	A/C DAMAGED	TRAINS	M. T.
S/L KIPP D.S.O. D.F.C. F/L OLDHAM	7 6	卐 卐 卐 卐 卐		卐 卐 卐 卐 卐	4	16
F/L COMPTON D.F.C. F/O MELLOY " "	9 9	卐 卐 卐 卐 卐	卐	卐 卐 卐 卐 卐 卐		3
F/L CRAFT D.F.C. F/O WATERS	6 7	卐 卐		卐 卐 卐 卐 卐 卐 卐 卐 卐 卐 卐 卐 卐 卐 卐 卐	2	
F/O LELONG D.F.C. F/O McLAREN D.F.C.	9 9	卐 卐 卐 卐 卐 卐 卐 卐		卐 卐 卐 卐 卐 卐 卐 卐 卐 卐 卐 卐 卐 卐 卐	3	5
F/L WILLIAMS D.F.C. KILLED F/L RICHARDS "	2 2	卐 卐				
F/O PANTER D.S.O. EX P.O.W. F/O SHARPLES D.F.C. KILLED	1 1	卐 卐 卐 卐 卐	卐	卐	1	
F/L WALKER KILLED F/O HUMBLESTONE "	1 1					
F/L MILLER D.F.C. ATT. F.I.U.S. KILLED F/O BARCLAY EX P.O.W.	1 1	卐		卐 卐		
F/L FOSTER ATTACHED FROM 25 SQN F/O PEARCE	1 1			卐		
F/L GRIFFIN " 456 " F/L WILLIAMS	1 1			卐		
F/O STRUTHERS " 151 " F/O COOPER	1 1			卐 卐 卐		
F/O LEDWIDGE " 25 " W/O BONNER	1 1					
TOTAL	40	28	2	50	10	24

CUCKFIELD RURAL DISTRICT

52. **Highbeeches House, Handcross, was demolished by a crippled RAF Halifax which crashed on to it on 12th March 1943.**

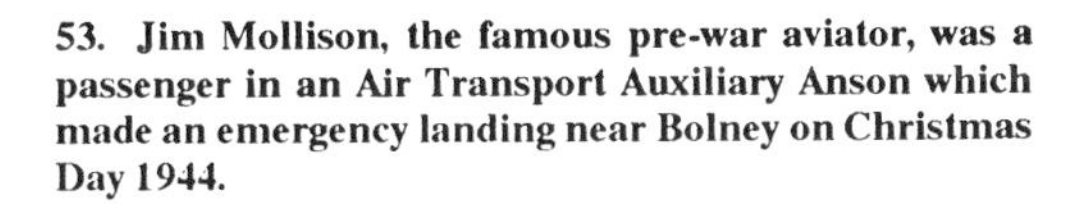

53. **Jim Mollison, the famous pre-war aviator, was a passenger in an Air Transport Auxiliary Anson which made an emergency landing near Bolney on Christmas Day 1944.**

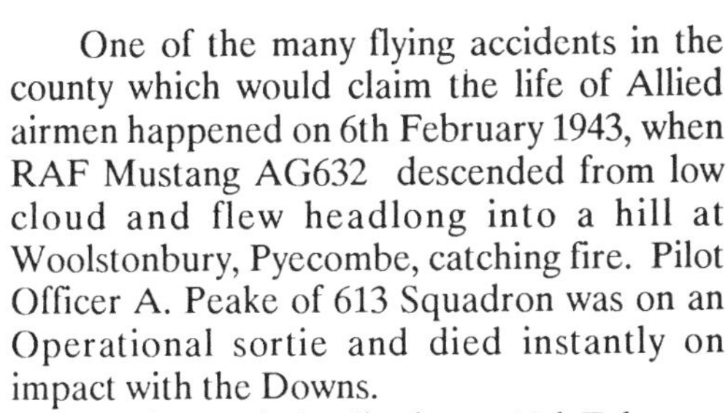

One of the many flying accidents in the county which would claim the life of Allied airmen happened on 6th February 1943, when RAF Mustang AG632 descended from low cloud and flew headlong into a hill at Woolstonbury, Pyecombe, catching fire. Pilot Officer A. Peake of 613 Squadron was on an Operational sortie and died instantly on impact with the Downs.

Tragedy struck the district on 10th February when bombs hit "Meadowsweet" in Cuckfield Road, Hurstpierpoint, and killed Heather Lamb, the four year old daughter of Pastor and Mrs. Lamb. The Pastor himself was injured and a number of houses were damaged in the daylight raid involving Dornier 217 aircraft ranging over a wide area of Sussex.

A month later, however, it was a British bomber which brought death and destruction to the civilian population. On 12th March, a Halifax of 76 Squadron was hit and badly damaged over Stuttgart but managed to make the English coast before all eight crewmen abandoned the aeroplane shortly after 2.00 am. Unfortunately, the crewless aeroplane tumbled out of control and fell onto High Beeches,

Balcombe Lane, Handcross, the residence of Col. G. H. Loder, M. C, High Sheriff of Sussex. The building immediately burst into flames and was almost entirely gutted. Three domestic staff, Bertha Edwards, Grace Stratton and Lizzie Williams were all killed as they slept upstairs in their quarters.

On 16th March, a Spitfire crashed in flames at Bishopstone Farm, having been abandoned in flight by its Canadian pilot Sgt. Horace Packard of 416 Squadron, Kenley. This time, the damage was confined to an orchard.

Another Halifax, this time from 51 Squadron, came down in the district after returning damaged from an attack on Gelsenkirchen on 10th July. At 04.22 hrs the bombers three running engines fell silent for lack of fuel - the main tanks having been holed over the target. Low over Balcombe the Halifax struck the top of an oak tree, bringing the bomber down into an adjacent meadow at Sydnye Farm. Careering along for 80 yards the bomber then struck another tree and stopped, caught fire and broke up. By some miracle the five men on board were all unharmed, released themselves from the wreckage and walked to Old Hall, Staplefield, where they telephoned their home station. Two men, though, were unaccounted for at the time having baled out over Germany when the bomber was hit. It was presumed they were Prisoners of War.

The year 1944 was notable for this district in that , on 13th June, the second flying bomb in England came down at Mizbrooks Farm, Cuckfield, causing damage but no casualties. (Only seven minutes earlier the first had fallen at Swanscombe, Kent.) This was the opening salvo of a terrible ordeal for the people of Southern England and one which would see 20 of these weapons falling in the Cuckfield Rural District area. Fortunately, and although much damage was caused, nobody in the area was killed during the flying bomb period.

An American Dakota aircraft was lost on 17th October when it crashed into Fulking Hill during stormy weather and poor visibility. Rescuers arriving on the scene found the aeroplane wrecked and burning fiercely with both engines thrown some 50 ft in front of the main body of the plane. Two men had been thrown clear but killed, and another body was pulled from the wreckage. When the flames finally subsided the fourth occupant was found in the wreckage. All four men were conveyed to a temporary mortuary established at The Royal Oak, Poynings. They added to the grim tally of over 50 Allied servicemen killed in no less than five separate identical incidents involving Dakota aircraft crashing into Sussex Downland.

The landing of an Avro Anson at Brooklands Farm, Muttons Corner, Bolney on Christmas Day 1944, was interesting in view of a notable passenger! Returning from Liberated Europe for Christmas celebrations at home the Air Transport Auxiliary "taxi" Anson was forced to land due to frost and fog and lst Officer Fairley put down without mishap. Two passengers were on board and one of them was Flight Captain Jim Mollison the famous pre-war aviator and husband of Amy Johnson. Forced to continue their journey to White Waltham by rail the three left the Anson in the charge of an inebriated band of Royal Irish Fusiliers who had been disturbed from their seasonal festivities at nearby Wighurst Park.

When it came to reckon up the total cost on VE Day it was found that 10 civilians had died through enemy action, three had died later in hospital and a number of others were seriously injured. Fifteen houses were destroyed and 716 damaged - the result of 618 high explosive bombs, 10,000 incendiaries and 20 Flying Bombs which all fell during some 1,896 air raid alerts in the Cuckfield Rural District area.

CUCKFIELD URBAN DISTRICT

The valuable work of Hurstwood Park War Emergency Hospital continued to save the lives of seriously injured air raid victims drawn from a catchment area across the whole of Southern England, including London. How many lives were saved it is impossible to say - sadly, only a roll of those who did not pull through survives to tell just part of the story. That roll, however, reflects the various peaks of enemy air activity - The Blitz, Hit & Run Raids, Operation Steinbock ("The Little Blitz") and, finally, the V1 and V2 attacks.

The Hospital, however, had a narrow escape when, on 26th June 1943, a tail-less Spitfire was seen to emerge from the clouds in a spiral dive - heading, it seemed, straight for the main buildings. As it descended, the pilot baled out and at the last moment the aeroplane veered slightly to narrowly miss the hospital and crash to earth by the base of a large tree in the grounds. Fg. Off. Robert Bowen of 403 Squadron was obliged to abandon his aeroplane when it had been rammed from behind by a Spitfire flown by his C.O, Sqn. Ldr. H.C. Godefroy DFC, causing complete loss of control as the tail section was severed. Sustaining a broken right arm on landing, Bower did not have far to go for emergency treatment! After medical attention, he was then taken to 14th Canadian General Hospital, Horley, leaving the Hurstwood Park staff every bit as shaken by this episode as he no doubt was.

One Flying Bomb fell in the district on 11th July 1944, exploding in the grounds of Haywards Heath Cemetery and damaging nearby properties.

During the whole period of the war only one civilian was seriously injured and 16 slightly injured in air raids. No-one was killed, but three houses were destroyed and damage caused to 602 others.

54. Canadian Squadron Leader H. C. Godefroy, DFC, and his Spitfire, marked with three German Aircraft "kills". On 26th June 1943, he accidentally destroyed a Spitfire after ramming it from behind in mid air, causing it to crash in the grounds of Hurstwood Park Hospital.

EASTBOURNE COUNTY BOROUGH

So far, Eastbourne had lived up to its grim reputation of being the most raided town in the South East and as 1943 opened it was clear the reputation was here for the duration of this war.

On 15th January the dreaded Focke Wulf 190's were back again and hit Wilmington Terrace, Devonshire Place, Cross Street, Duke Street and Langney Road killing at least ten people.

On 7th February a serious blow was struck when yet more Focke Wulf 190's dropped several bombs - one of which demolished the Central Fire Station killing five firemen and one firewoman. In addition, nine members of the general public were killed in this raid as well as four soldiers.

On 11th February, a Spitfire of 611 Squadron hit the sea and crashed whilst low flying South of Beachy Head. Sgt. A. E. Pearce, who had been on a patrol, was posted "missing".

The full story of Eastbourne's ordeal by bomb and gunfire has already been told elsewhere and the sheer number and scale of attacks would make a full accounting of each quite impossible in this volume. However, there are some which are worthy of note. The 3rd April was one such case.

On this date the town experienced its worst ever casualty figures for a single raid as ten assorted fighter bombers delivered their deadly cargoes. Bombs hit widespread parts of the town and at least fourteen persons were killed in a surface air raid shelter at Spencer Road which was hit by a bomb completely destroying it. Elsewhere, bombs hit Terminus Road, Longstone Road, Avondale Road and Compton Street and when the total death toll was taken 35 were dead and 99 injured.

On 4th June, 18 Focke Wulf 190's approached Beachy Head at "zero" feet, climbed up over the headland and wheeled round to bomb the town as they returned back out to sea. Inevitably, the devastation was considerable and the raid left seven dead and fifteen injured. Five service personnel were also injured although anti-aircraft fire and fighter aircraft were in action claiming the destruction of one of the raiders at Normans Bay (See Hailsham Rural District). St. Saviours Church had a remarkable escape from destruction when a bomb hit the vicarage and went on through the Church roof coming to rest in the pews without exploding.

Two days later the same Luftwaffe unit was back to terrorise the town - this time with fourteen Focke Wulf 190's. One of the pilots, Lt. Helmut Wenk of II/SKG10 takes up the story:

"As we neared Eastbourne we shifted from our cruising formation (line abreast) into our attack formation - line astern. At the same time we opened to full throttle and flying about 30 ft above the sea. Just before we crossed the coast we climbed to 900 ft and turned in to attack. Plunging down through the flak we released our bombs in a "turnip-lob" shallow dive attack then got down to low level and curved round to port to escape round the back of Beachy Head and out to sea."

Once again there was widespread damage and the "turnip-lob" of Hemut Wenk and Co. had cost the lives of at least seven civilians and several military policemen. As they passed out to sea the raiders shot up the ROC post on Beachy Head in a parting gesture. It was, however, the last raid on this scale and the worst of Eastbourne's air raid ordeal was over. Tragedy befell the two crew of a Defiant nightfighter of 515 Squadron which flew headlong into the Downs near Beachy Head Hotel on 8th June in fog. This accident was attributed in part to the Ground Controller at Tangmere. On 11th August it was an engine fire which caused the crash of a 64 Squadron Spitfire at Langney. Fortunately, the pilot walked away from this one.

On the night of 8th/9th November a Messerschmitt 410 bomber was sent into a screaming vertical dive over the town after an attack by nightfighter. Trailing fire and sparks the bomber impacted at Shinewater Marsh, Hampden Park, and exploded violently, - blasting a massive crater in the soft soil. Research could readily identify the victors as Squadron Leader "Bill" Maguire and Fg. Off. W.D. Jones who were flying in a Mosquito of 85 Squadron. More difficult to ascertain was the identity of the Me.410 crew as several were lost that night and the two men in this aeroplane were never identified and never buried. In the 1970s , however, investigations of the crash site revealed a small plate bearing the number 10244, enabling the identity of the aeroplane to be established and linked to its crew - Major Wilhelm Schmitter and Uffz. Felix Hainzinger. The Major was highly decorated, holding the Knights Cross with Oakleaves - the highest German award for valour. Both men remain unaccounted for.

2nd February 1944, saw the loss of a B-24 Liberator returning from a bombardment of the "V" weapon sites then being built in Northern France. Having become lost in cloud the pilot, lst Lt. James Bolin, gingerly brought his four engined bomber down through the cloud to seek a landing place. Unfortunately, as he descended he ran straight into the Downs above the Golf Course at Ratton and missed clearing the brow by a matter of feet. The huge bomber, which carried the name "Ruth-less" on its nose, was scattered in pieces across the hillside with the broken bodies of its ten crew strewn amidst the burning debris. Remarkably, two of the ten men survived the impact but died later in hospital. Although the people of Eastbourne had no way of knowing it, these ten young "Yanks" had died on a mission to help spare the civilians of Britain from the anticipated horrors of attack by V1 Flying Bombs.

When they came the V1 attacks hit Eastbourne hard and with the ever present threat of the bomb motor cutting out overhead, the weapon being hit by anti aircraft gunfire or intercepted by a fighter. It was the latter scenario which caused extensive damage to Astaire Avenue on 4th July when a bomb was shot down by fighter aircraft. Remarkably, there were no fatal casualties. At the end of the Flying Bomb attacks fifteen had fallen in the Borough causing extensive damage.

As the war drew to a close a Dakota aircraft of the USAAF crashed within a few yards of the spot where the Defiant had been wrecked in June 1943. Catching fire on impact, one of the crew was dragged out by RAF, Police and Observer Corps personnel despite the intense heat. One other crewman was thrown clear and lived to tell the tale. Despite extensive research it has not been possible to identify the date, details or crew of this aeroplane incident. Perhaps a reader can shed some light?

The cost to Eastbourne had certainly been high, and in view its dubious claim to fame as "Most Raided Town" the detailed official statistics are reproduced here.

55. **This was the scene of desolation at the bottom of Grove Road, Eastbourne, immediately after the air raid on 4th June 1943.**

ALERTS	1350	FLYING BOMBS	15
LOCAL ALERTS (IMINENT DANGER)	861	SHELLS	1
INCIDENTS	112	CRASHED ENEMY AIRCRAFT	5
H.E. BOMBS	671	MACHINE GUN AND CANNON -	20
U.X.B.	76	FIRE INCIDENTS	
OIL BOMBS	28	MINES (SEA) GERMAN	13
INCENDIARY BOMBS (APPROX. NO.)	4000	BRITISH	5
PHOSPHORUS BOMBS	5	UNIDENTIFIED	3
PHOSPHORUS BOMBS (UNEXPLODED)	3	OTHER MISSILES	NIL

Many other bombs fell in the sea which are not included in the above figures.

Three Flying Bombs fell outside the area and caused damage within the Local Authority area.

CASUALTIES CIVILIAN 1106

	INCIDENTS	DEAD			INJURED AND DETAINED			INJURED OTHER CASES			MISSING		
		M.	W.	C.	M.	W.	C.	M.	W.	C.	M.	W.	C.
1940-1	71	22	13	1	49	85	8	58	75	6			
1942	10	18	27	7	46	42	12	41	52	5			
1943	10	26	54	4	51	77	7	67	89	14	1	1	
1944	11				18	41	7	33	42	7			
TOTALS	102	66	94	12	164	245	34	199	258	32	1	1	
			172			443			489			2	

CASUALTIES FROM FLYING BOMBS. Died following admission to hospital. 41.

DEAD	INJURED & DETAINED IN HOSPITAL	INJURED OTHER CASES
NIL	62	79

SERVICE CASUALTIES 183

	DEAD			INJURED AND DETAINED			INJURED OTHER CASES		
	M.	W.	C.	M.	W.	C.	M.	W.	C.
1942	8			2			7	1	
1943	15	1		46	8		55	17	
1944	4			7			11	1	
	27	1		55	8		73	19	

DAMAGE TO PROPERTY Died following admission to hospital. 5.

HOUSES DESTROYED	475
SERIOUSLY DAMAGED	1,000
SLIGHTLY DAMAGED	10,000

LOCAL AUTHORITY EASTBOURNE

A.R.P. Controller

DATE 6.12.44.

56. The Metropole Hotel on Eastbourne sea front was demolished by a direct hit on 4th June 1943. A block of flats called Metropole Court now occupies the site.

57. On 4th June 1943, a 500Kg bomb came to rest in St. Saviours Church, Eastbourne, and failed to explode. This is the Bomb Disposal clearance certificate for the St. Saviours bomb.

PART IV.

CLEARANCE CERTIFICATE SERIAL No. 54686 EAST/

THE UNEXPLODED BOMB/XXX in St. Saviour's Church, Eastbourne

HAS (~~HAVE~~) NOW BEEN (a) Disposed of

~~(b) Discredited.~~

~~(c) Abandoned.~~

2. TIME. 1200 DATE. 7 JUN. 43

Good!! 6/43 29

SIGNED. O. Behrendt

RANK. MAJOR. RE. Major, R.E.

UNIT. O.C. No. 29 Bomb Disposal Coy. R.E.

*(16442D Wt 20725/350 5000 7/42 H J R & L Gp 745/6

58. On 8th/9th November 1943, Sqn. Ldr. W. Maguire and Fg. Off. W.D. Jones, in a Mosquito of 85 Squadron, shot down a Messerschmitt 410 onto marshland near Hampden Park. In August, 1976, parts of the Messerschmitt were recovered, with Mr. W. D. Jones in attendance. He was then Headmaster of Ticehurst C.P.School and is shown here holding one of the Me.410's propeller blades. (Your authors are on the left).

59. Fg. Off. W.D. Jones was Navigator of the Mosquito and is pictured here with the aeroplane at RAF West Malling in 1943.

60. The crumpled tail is the only recognisable part left from the B-24 Liberator which hit the Downs above Ratton on 2nd February 1944, with the loss of all ten crew.

61. An American Officer, Policemen, ARP Warden and British soldiers examine the jet pipe of a V1 Flying Bomb which exploded on 18th June 1944, laying to waste a large area of Charlestone, Milton and Mountney Roads.

62. At Astaire Avenue, Eastbourne, there was extensive damage caused by another V1 shot down there on 4th July 1944.

63. On 8th June 1943, a Defiant nightfighter flew headlong into the Downs by the Beachy Head Hotel in thick fog. Both crew were killed.

EAST GRINSTEAD URBAN DISTRICT

Just one event dominates the story of the war in East Grinstead - the bombing of the Whitehall Cinema on 19th July 1943. It proved to be the worst air raid disaster of the war for the county of Sussex and killed at least 108 people. (The second worst air raid disaster in Sussex also involved bombing of a cinema, the Odeon at Kemp Town, Brighton, where 55 people died on 14th September 1940.)

On this dull Friday in the school summer holidays it was only to be expected that many children would be in the town's cinema situated on London Road, and if there was an air raid warning then it is clear that few people paid any heed. Suddenly, a Dornier 217 slipped out of the hazy clouds, circled the town and then ran in to drop eight bombs across London Road and the High Street. The destruction and carnage that ensued can only be described as horrendous, with many buildings simply collapsing into heaps of burning rubble. Worst of all, though, was the scene at the Whitehall Cinema where one of the bombs had exploded in the auditorium, collapsing walls, girders and the roof dome onto the packed audience. Whole families were wiped out in some cases and, in many instances, no tangible trace could be located of some of the victims. Others, dead or dying, had been blasted into the street outside while some bodies had been flung grotesquely into the twisted roof girders. Meanwhile, fire began to spread rapidly from building to building as dazed survivors, - many bleeding from flying glass injuries, - staggered helplessly about the streets. The fires, the debris, the bodies and the injured or shocked all presented what one witness could only describe as " a vision from Hell, and one of sheer and unimaginable horror".

As a cloud of black and yellow sulphurous smoke hung over the town the grim body count began - it ended at 108 dead, but that may not be the total figure. At least 235 were injured, some seriously. However, it is known that the cinema could seat 400 and that as least 184 were in the auditorium at the time. The actual figure will probably never be known, but 22 of the victims were buried in a communal grave at Mount Noddy, East Grinstead, where the marker stones provide a grim reminder of East Grinstead's darkest hour.

When the Flying Bomb attacks began in 1944 one of the V1s fell, incredibly, on exactly the same spot and exploded in the rubble of the cinema. In this incident three people were killed, 38 injured and over 400 properties were damaged including a number of shops which were totally destroyed. Within hours of this Vl falling, their Majesties the King and Queen visited the town, inspected the damage and met with the Civil Defence and emergency services workers.

The last V1 came down as late as 25th March 1945, and was one of the very last to fall in the entire country. It exploded in the North End area and although casualties were extremely light, damage to property was extensive.

VE Day celebrations in East Grinstead on 8th May 1945, were naturally tinged with sadness and grief still felt for the Whitehall Cinema tragedy. Even with the passage of fifty years it still remains a painful memory for hundreds of people.

64. Before and after. This was London Road, East Grinstead, during the 1920's (Whitehall Cinema on the left).

65. This is almost the same view after a German bomber had passed on 9th July 1943, leaving 108 dead. (In this picture, the Cinema is just out of the picture to the left.)

66. This was the remains of the Whitehall Cinema with its walls and domed roof having collapsed bodily into the auditorium.

67. There are claims that the Dornier 217 responsible for bombing East Grinstead was later shot down. If so, it is possible that it was the machine shot down at Detling, Kent, and shown here.

68. Alternatively it may have been the aeroplane shot down on the same day at Bletchingley, Surrey. In 1970, unexploded bombs were found in the wreckage of the Dornier.

69. Obergefreiter Karl Dubiak was one of the four crew killed in the Bletchingley Dornier. Was this fresh-faced young boy one of the East Grinstead bombers?

70. Queen Victoria Hospital, East Grinstead, where pioneering plastic surgery was performed on badly burned and injured air crew. Casualties from the Whitehall Cinema bombing were also treated here.

71. The King and Queen visited East Grinstead on 12th July 1944, just a few hours after a V1 had exploded on the town, and chatted to Civil Defence workers.

HAILSHAM RURAL DISTRICT

On the 23rd January 1943 Hailsham's good fortune was an ill-wind for Polegate which found itself on the receiving end of an attack meant for Hailsham, four miles to the north. Instead, a raiding force of Focke Wulf 190's dropped bombs across Southlands housing estate having made a navigational error. One bomb hit a pair of semi-detached houses, 17-19 Western Avenue, killing Margaret Bridger, Caroline Thorpe and Gunner Stanley Gifford of the Royal Canadian Artillery. One of the raiding aircraft was shot down by light anti-aircraft fire as it sped out across Beachy Head, its pilot killed when the aircraft crashed into the sea.

Having had a fortunate escape on 23rd January, Hailsham had its turn three weeks later when, on 10th February, a single Dornier 217 slipped out of low overcast and dropped two high explosive bombs on the town. One bomb exploded on the railway cutting near Clifton House, Western Road, and the other crashed through the roof of a garage at the rear of the Post Office in North Street, shed its fins and bounced 300 yards across the town to explode behind St. Mary's Church in Vicarage Lane. Most of the stained glass windows were blown out of the Parish Church and a newly erected NFS Fire Station was wrecked but there were only a few casualties, none of them fatal. Despite the damage, Hailsham had again had a remarkable deliverance!

On 4th June 1943, Focke Wulf 190 aircraft attacking Eastbourne were heavily engaged by anti-aircraft fire and by Spitfires of 41 Squadron based at Friston. One of the raiders was hit and crashed near the Star Inn, Normans Bay, flipping over onto its back as it had attempted to land and, in doing so, struck the banks of a drainage ditch. The pilot, Oberleutnant Kurt Hevler, was killed.

Just a short distance away, on 11th August, an RAF four engined Stirling bomber ditched in the sea at Normans Bay. Two of the crew were drowned, but the others were plucked to safety by Rescue Launch. Steadily, the numbers of allied bomber aircraft which crashed in the county would rise as the bombing offensive against Occupied Europe and Germany gathered momentum. Many returning bombers, crippled or short of fuel, staggered across the English coast. Others came to grief en-route to their targets. On 6th September the district was awash with returning B-17 Flying Fortresses. One came down on the foreshore at Pevensey, six landed at Friston aerodrome and nineteen others at RAF Deanland near Golden Cross.

Another crippled bomber, this time an RAF Halifax, crashed into woodland at Heathfield Park, close to the Gibraltar Tower. Returning damaged from a raid on Frankfurt, six of the crew baled out safely but two others had been killed when the aeroplane was hit over Germany. Their bodies were discovered in the burnt wreckage.

It was outgoing bombers, however, which were involved in a terrible tragedy on the 31st August when two B-17 Flying Fortresses collided off Beachy Head. One of the aeroplanes, named "Eager Eagle", was sliced in two by another, "Snooks", which also went down into the sea. Altogether, at least eleven airman were killed, although four parachutes were seen descending from "Eager Eagle". Debris from the two bombers then struck another Fortress, "L'il Audrey", which turned inland and crashed at Wooton Manor, Polegate, mowing down a row of trees and catching fire. Eight of the men on board were killed, but two were found away from the wreckage and admitted to hospital in Eastbourne. Police Constable E. Page and Sgt. C. Hopkins were awarded British Empire Medals for forcing an entry into the burning wreck in order to ascertain that no one was trapped. They were hampered by terrific heat and explosions of ammunition and flares, and also by a burning tree trunk which had fallen onto the fuselage. According to the citation for award of the medals the two Police Officers ".....showed courage and devotion to duty without regard for their own safety ." It had been a catastrophe, though, for the 91st Bomb Group to whom all of the aeroplanes and crews belonged.

On 17th October a lull of 93 days during which no enemy bomb had fallen in daylight on England was broken as two bombs were dropped in fields at Grovelands Farm, Hailsham. Huge craters were blown in the ground, but there were no casualties and very little damage was caused.

Armistice day 1943 (11th November), saw a tragedy involving an RAF P-51 Mustang which caught fire in mid air while flying inland from the coast and crashed at Horselunges Farm, Hellingly, on the boundary of Hellingly Cemetery. The young pilot, Flying Officer Peter Hay-Neave, was killed as the Mustang exploded on impact.

On the last day of the year, a P47 Thunderbolt of the USAAF crash landed at Rockhouse Bank, Normans Bay, out of fuel following a long range bomber escort mission. Although lucky to have made landfall the pilot sustained severe facial injuries when he was thrown forward onto the gunsight.

Equally fortunate to survive was Flt. Sgt. Moureau, a Belgian Spitfire pilot serving with 349 Squadron at Friston, who escaped a forced landing at Herstmonceux four days into the New Year. Two weeks later, on 21st January German night raiders were back and a random bomb at "Tweenways", East Hoathly, killed Christabel Goodhart and nine year old Michael Goodhart, the wife and son of Group Captain Jack Goodhart, RAF. On the 14th March 1944, a night raider was shot down at Friston, the Dornier 217 diving vertically to earth near the RAF station, exploding, and killing all four crew. By dawn, little remained apart from molten metal and the charred remains of a parachute.

On 29th April it was again the turn of Belgian pilot Moureau (now a Pilot Officer) to come to grief in his Spitfire. This time he crashed near Friston Aerodrome and was seriously injured, his plane being written off at Gate Field.

The onset of the Flying Bomb campaign in June 1944, saw one of the most frightening and traumatic periods of the war for the district which opened at 4.00am on 16th June as one of the missiles exploded at Riversdale Nursery, Marle Green. There were no casualties this time, but it was the first of 159 Flying Bombs down in the Rural District area and there would yet be widespread casualties and extensive damage to property.

Defence against these weapons involved fighter aircraft and anti-aircraft guns, both with the objective of knocking the Flying Bombs from the sky and preventing them from reaching London, their intended target. However, this resulted in an often heavy price for the people of Sussex and Kent. Notwithstanding the fact that much of the area where these Flying Bombs were intercepted was over open country they could, all the same, still have a disastrous effect if bought down. For example, on 4th July an RAF Tempest shot down a Flying Bomb at Windyridge, Maynards Green, killing Edith Campbell and injuring ten others. Other methods of engaging V1s were also tried by RAF pilots, including tipping the missiles over with their aircraft wing-tip air flow. On July 7th this resulted in four deaths at Polegate. On the same day, at Arlington, a woman was killed when her house, "Placketts", was destroyed by a falling bomb - this time it was the result of the engine simply cutting out and the device falling to earth. On the 10th, Richard Barnes and Freda Goldsmith were killed as they worked at Mulbrooks Farm, Hailsham - the blast from a V1 toppling a hayrick onto them. Yet again , on the 23rd, fighters brought down a V1 and caused civilian fatalities - this time two people being killed at Camberlot Road, Lower Dicker. The price of defending London was surely high.

The Flying Bomb campaign seemed to continue relentlessly, but the last fatalities were at Laughton on 4th August where five people were killed and the sub-post office, two cottages and The Bell Inn were all destroyed.

Well used to the warning "throb" of an approaching V1 the population of the area were shaken by a truly massive bang in the sky over Willingdon which came without warning on 19th September. The thunderclap explosion seemed that it must have torn Willindgdon apart. This was a V2 rocket which had exploded in mid air and, fortunately, caused no serious damage or casualties. Launched against London from Holland this rocket was way off-track and seems to have been the furthest south that a V2 is recorded as having fallen.

On the 30th of the month an RAF B25 Mitchell bomber, laden with stores, caught fire in flight over Sussex. Items of cargo were dumped on a line from Haywards Heath to Chilley Bridge, Pevensey, where the bomber crashed into the River Haven after being abandoned by its three crew, one of whom was killed. In 1970 one of the Wright Cyclone engines and two propeller assemblies were salvaged from the river by an RAF diving team.

Although by 1945, aerial activity was on the

decline over Sussex as the Allied armies rolled on across Europe one of the worst wartime air disasters in the County was yet to happen. On 6th February a DC-3 Dakota transport crashed into the South Downs near Folkington in thick fog, killing all 23 service personnel on board. By strange coincidence another Dakota suffered the same fate nearby and under similar circumstances when it struck the Downs near the Long Man, on 6th May. All four occupants were killed. Two days later the war in Europe was over.

For Hailsham Rural District the war had left 27 civilians dead, 300 injured, 52 houses destroyed, 5,000 houses damaged, 1,355 high explosive bombs and 230 anti-personnel bombs across 31 individual parishes. Add to this the 159 Flying Bombs, one V2 Rocket, thousands of incendiaries and scores of downed aeroplanes, Allied and Enemy, and the scale of events is put into perspective.

72. One of the FW.190's which bombed Polegate on 23rd January 1943, was shot down into the sea off Holywell. Uffz. Alfred Immervoll was killed.

73. One of the sleek new Spitfire XIV's of 41 Squadron at RAF Friston in 1943. These fighters helped to counter the menace of the Focke Wulf 190 Hit and Run attacks.

74. **This was how the Bexhill on Sea Observer reported the shooting down of the FW. 190 at Normans Bay on 4th June 1943. Unusually for a wartime newspaper the location of the incident was given.**

SATURDAY, JUNE 12, 1943

END OF A SNEAK RAIDER

Good shooting. This F.W. 190, seen lying on its back, was brought down by Ack-Ack fire at Norma
Bay during a recent raid on the South-East Coast.

Some of the gun crew, who shot down the plane, examining the wreckage.

75. A B-24 Liberator burns at RAF Friston after crashing on 12th March 1944.

76. Soldiers and an RAF Officer sift through the pitiful remains of a Dornier 217 shot down at Friston on 14th March 1944. This view is taken looking into the Cuckmere Valley.

77. John Davis (left) and Reg Burgess (father of co-author Pat Burgess) with the jet pipe of a V1 "Doodlebug" which exploded in Isenhurst Wood, Heathfield, during the summer of 1944. Pat also had some first-hand " Doodlebug " experience, being blown clean off his feet by one which exploded in Heathfield Park!

78. An RAF Diving Team work on the salvage of a B-25 Mitchell from the River Haven, Chilley Bridge, in October 1970. The crater gouged out by the bomber can be seen on the far bank. It crashed here on 30th September 1944.

79. Only the rocket motor survived when a V2 exploded over Willingdon on 19th September 1944.

80. The Friston based Belgian pilots of 349 Squadron. Flt. Sgt. Moureau, (reclining on the Spitfire cowling) crashed twice in the Hailsham Rural District area. Henri Limet, in the Spitfire cockpit, baled out over Battle on 30th January 1944. (See Battle Rural District)

81. When the Home Guard stood down in November 1944, all those who served were presented with certificates of recognition. Philip Bear had served as an Officer with 20th (Sussex) Hailsham Battalion.

In the years when our Country

was in mortal danger

Philip Kingsbury Bear

who served *May 1940 to December 1944.*

gave generously of his time and

powers to make himself ready

for her defence by force of arms

and with his life if need be.

George R.I.

THE HOME GUARD

HASTINGS COUNTY BOROUGH

The year 1943 was to see the heaviest air attacks of the war for Hastings, the year beginning with raids on 9th, 17th and 20th January. It was not until 11th March, however, that the town suffered its worst air raid of the war. In this attack 25 high explosive bombs were dropped by several waves of Fock Wulf 190 aircraft sweeping in from the North, dropping their loads and machine gunning the town on their escape out to sea. It was primarily the Silverhill district which suffered the most, with shops, houses and St. Matthews School (fortunately empty) all being destroyed. The death toll was high, with 38 persons killed, 39 seriously injured and 51 injured. One week later, on the 16th, HRH the Duchess of Kent visited the town, saw the damage and chatted with survivors and people who had lost their homes. She also met with representatives of all the emergency and Civil Defence services and saw Hastings unique natural air raid shelter - St Clements Caves. It was a visit which cheered the townspeople and raised morale. Everyone was struck by the genuine concern of the Duchess, herself in deep mourning for HRH the Duke of Kent who had recently been killed serving in the RAF.

Shortly before 1.00pm on Sunday, 23rd May, a further heavy attack was launched by another force of Focke Wulf 190's in which 25 bombs were also dropped. This time it was the Old Town, Seafront, and London Road areas which were badly hit and a total of 25 people were killed and 85 injured. A number of Canadian Soldiers were killed in their billet at The Albany Hotel on the seafront by a bomb which had ricocheted off the nearby Queens Hotel and then demolished the Albany. A block of flats (Albany Court) and part of Debenhams store now stand on the site. The raid was also noticeable in that no less than five hotels and pubs were hit in this attack - most of them packed with Sunday lunchtime drinkers.

On 6th June 1943, a Spitfire of 91 Squadron developed engine problems whilst on patrol over the town and the pilot, Fg. Off. H. Johnson, was forced to make an emergency landing at St. Helens Road. In a bumpy crash to earth Johnson was injured about the head and admitted to the Royal East Sussex Hospital. The Spitfire, number EN622, was repaired and returned to service - as was Fg. Off. Johnson! In a subsequent Air Ministry report on the incident it was stated "Johnson, as a pilot, was first class. He saved lives by making an excellent landing in a field surrounded by houses".

Another fighter loss resulting from engine failure happened on 21st October. This time, an RAF Typhoon was involved and the pilot, Fg. Off. E. Bater of 245 Squadron, baled out but was killed. His was one of many many crashes of aircraft, allied and enemy, which took place at sea just offshore from Hastings. Even now, fifty years on, the Hastings fishing fleet regularly trawls up engines, propellers and other aeronautical debris left over from these episodes. One such "catch" during the 1970s by fishing vessel RX 59 was the massive undercarriage assembly of a Heinkel 177. This was left over from the crash of one of these unusual aeroplanes just offshore on 22nd January 1944. Hit by a 85 Squadron Mosquito nightfighter flown by Fg. Off. Nowell and Sgt. Randell, only two of the crew survived, having parachuted into Hastings where they were captured. Fw. Beitter and Ofw. Andrae were the observer and flight engineer respectively and were the only survivors out of a crew of six. Andrae, it is recorded, could tell his interrogators nothing since he was suffering from concussion - a convenient and plausible excuse which doubtless frustrated his captors considerably! Of the other crewmen, one body was washed ashore at Dover and another at Lydd. There has never been any trace of the other two.

The area around Emmanuel Church was hit again (see also *Blitz over Sussex 1941-42*) during the early hours of 12th March, and nos 22 and 24 Priory Road took a direct hit. The houses were almost opposite the church and rescuers toiled by moonlight to extricate the victims. At the end of their grim search the body count was five, with 70 year old artist Leslie Badham and his daughter, Dorothy, being killed at 22 and George and Ethel Saunders and their five year old son, Bryon, dead at number 24.

Three days into the Flying Bomb attacks one

of these fiendish devices was hit by anti-aircraft gunfire and exploded onto the south bank of the railway line at Glyne Gap. Widespread but superficial damage was caused to houses in the Bexhill Road area although worse was yet to come in the weeks which followed. In total, fifteen V1s came down in the Borough and at least four people were killed as a result. St. Leonards Parish Church at Marina was totally destroyed when a V1 exploded on the steps of the building, razing it to the ground. Also at St.Leonards, on the seafront at Sea Road, a battery of seven heavy 3.7 inch anti-aircraft guns was established and put up a fearsome barrage at any approaching V1s. On West Hill, 481 Bty, Royal Artillery, was a "mixed" unit of regular soldiers and ATS girls - one of who's number was Miss Mary Churchill, the Prime Ministers daughter. Rather ignominiously, the Battery Command Post was situated in the Ladies public lavatory at the top of the Cliff Railway!. Another means of defence against the Flying Bomb menace were regular standing patrols of fighter aircraft and, on 19th June, a Spitfire of 322 Sgn, RAF, went into the sea off Hastings seafront after its engine cut out on a V1 interception patrol. Sgt.E.Veiersted (of Norway) baled out uninjured from his Spitfire, MK341.

Another loss of an aircraft on a V1 patrol involved a Mosquito of 125 Sqn on 21st August, when HK 291 was shot down by our own Anti-Aircraft fire and crashed into the sea off the town.

When the war in Europe was at an end 154 persons had been killed in Hastings and St. Leonards during air attacks and over 700 injured. No less than 1,463 air raid warnings were sounded - during which there were 85 actual attacks and 550 high explosive bombs dropped in the Borough. For many years the scars left by the loss of 463 properties demolished and 14,818 damaged were clearly visible in some parts of the town. Indeed, even now there are apparently unexplained gaps in rows of terraced houses or modern buildings looking out of place surrounded by old or ancient properties. Most often these are found to be the visible reminders of this Country's ordeal by bombing. Such reminders are everywhere to be seen in Hastings and St. Leonards.

82. This was Adelaide Road, Hastings, where several people were killed on 11th March 1943. The bombs narrowly missed a Police Station and it is interesting to note the two Policemen who take up a precarious perch whilst searching the rubble.

83. On 23rd May 1943, a fighter bomber attack was mounted against Hastings. One bomb entered a second floor window of the Queens Hotel (note groove in canopy top), exited by the side wall, passed across the street and through the second floor of the Albany Hotel where it exploded killing several Canadian soldiers. The Albany Hotel was demolished and Albany Court flats now stand on the spot.

84. "Monty" and his men! Field Marshal Montgomery addressing troops at Hastings during May 1944, in the great D-Day build up.

85. A battery of 3.7 inch heavy anti-aircraft guns on the promenade at Sea Road, West Marina, St. Leonards-on-Sea, to counter the V1 threat during the Summer of 1944.

86. A little further eastwards, at Glyne Gap, a battery of 40mm Bofors guns await the next flying bomb.

87. Hit by anti-aircraft gunfire, one V1 exploded on the railway embankment close to Bexhill Road, St. Leonards-on-Sea causing widespread damage to windows and roofs. Here, repair work gets underway and important beer deliveries to the Bull Inn are apparently not interupted! This spot has changed little, although the trolleybus wires have gone.

88. An unusual catch, this skeletal wing section was trawled up off Rye by Hastings fishermen in 1993. It originated from a B-17 Flying Fortress which crashed in 1945 after being abandoned by its ten crew.

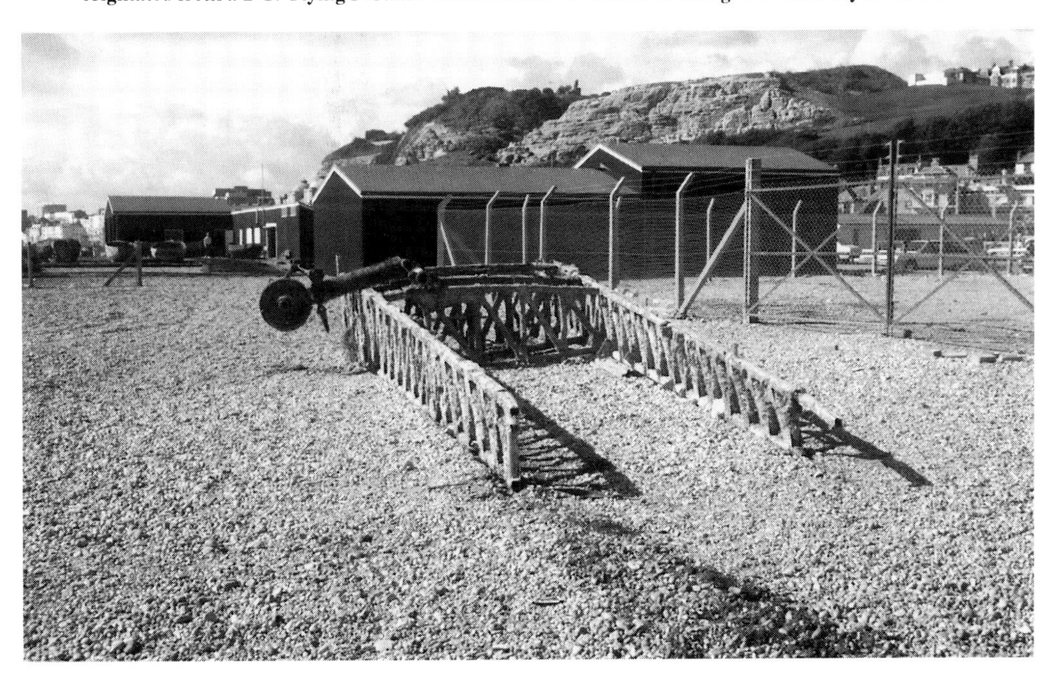

HORSHAM RURAL DISTRICT

Yet another school bombing tragedy could so easily have happened on 4th February 1943, when two bombs fell at West Green Church of England School at 8.30 am. Fortunately, no one was on the premises except the cleaner. He was uninjured although the school was extensively damaged

A few days later, though, it was a different story when bombs hit Station Road, Crawley, killing two elderly ladies, Ellen Carter and Elizabeth Cromwell. This was to be the last civilian loss of life until the flying bombs started to fall in 1944. Remarkably, there were no aircraft losses - Allied or enemy - until 6th December 1943, when a Spitfire which had been involved in a mid-air collision crashed at Colegate Road killing Fg. Off. F.D. Thomas of 91 Sqn. (See also Horsham Urban District reference this same incident). As regards to aircraft losses, it was a rather different story in 1944 when thirteen Allied and one enemy are recorded as having crashed.

The first of these incidents involved the collision and subsequent crash of two B-25 Mitchells at Pallinghurst, Rudgwick on 7th January when they were returning to their nearby Dunsfold base. Both 'planes fell close to Pallinghurst House - one 200 yards to the south, the other 200 yards to the north-east. The aeroplanes exploded and burnt, killing the four crew members in each aircraft and damaging a cottage and stables in Pallinghurst House grounds. (There was another similar incident involving B-25 Mitchells in 1944 within the Horsham Urban District area).

At Steep Wood Farm, Adversane, on 24th January Flt. Sgt. R. J.Wright had a lucky escape in a rather bumpy crash landing when his Hurricane's engine caught fire at 3,000 ft. Coming in to land the plane caught the tops of trees and dropped into a wheatfield, with the starboard wing digging into the ground and slewing the aircraft around. When it came to rest it was minus its propeller and tailwheel and generally battered and bent but Wright was unharmed.

The shooting down of a Messerschmitt 410 at Keepers Cottage, Nuthurst, on the night of 19th/20th April resulted in the death of the two crew, Lt. Witt and Uffz. Tesch, after they had been engaged by a Mosquito of 456 Squadron crewed by Flt. Lt. Brooks and W/O Forbes. The bomber went vertically into the ground at the edge of a copse on Cooks Farm, exploded and burnt out.

With preparations for the forthcoming D-Day invasion the presence of military hardware and personnel in the district became more and more apparent but, on 30th May 1944, part of the Allied battle plan was unwittingly dropped into the roadway at Buck Barn Cross Roads, West Grinstead, in the form of 36 maps of Northern France rolled up and tied with string. Found by 15 year old Derek Stevens, they were handed to the police with no harm done to Allied security. No doubt, though, there were serious recriminations for the driver of the jeep from which the maps had been allowed to so carelessly fall!

When the V1 Flying Bomb attacks started a number of these weapons fell in the district, but the most serious was at Crawley on the 10th July when one blew up at the junction of Oak Road and West Street killing 7 people and seriously injuring 44. Over 1,200 premises were damaged and 24 completely destroyed. On the same day, however, another V1 fell at Malthouse Road, Crawley, and failed to explode. Less dramatic was the landing of a Fairchild Argus communications aircraft at Appletree Farm, Ifield, on 20th August following engine trouble. The episode involved Mr Kenneth Wood, a pilot of the Air Transport Auxiliary which was the organisation responsible for ferrying aircraft of all types to operational units direct from factories and Maintenance Units. In this incident Mr. Wood was unhurt and returned to his home airfield at White Waltham.

The last aircraft down was also a communications aeroplane - this time a Percival Proctor. This crashed between Greathouse Farm and Southwater School, smashing off one wing and knocking down a telegraph pole.

The war came to an end with no other enemy action in the district and no other significant incident to report. However, on 8th May 1945, the civilian death toll stood at 14, but this rose to 15 on the 16th June 1945, with the death at Crawley of 42 year old Reginald Love who had been terribly injured by a crashing German bomber at Worth during October 1940.

89. Steve Hall (left) and Brian Connolly of the Wealden Aviation Archaeological Group excavate a propeller in 1976 at the Messerschmitt 410 crash site in Nuthurst. The bomber was shot down on 19th April, 1944.

90. This scorched wallet was found at the edge of the copse where the Nuthurst Messerschmitt 410 crashed. It contained one German and one Danish coin and a teddy bear lucky charm.

91. Squadron Leader Horbaczewski, DSO, The Polish CO of 315 Squadron at RAF Coolham. On one notable occasion Horbaczewski landed his Mustang in France and picked up a fellow pilot who had force-landed, flying back to Coolham with the other man sitting on his lap in the single seat aeroplane! (Note the bomb mission tallies, aircraft "kills" and four V1 victories marked on the Mustang).

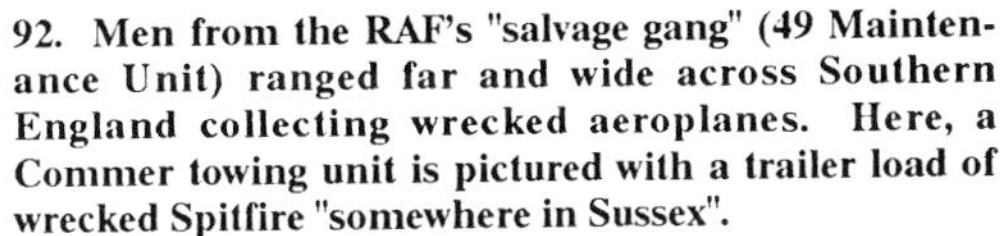

92. Men from the RAF's "salvage gang" (49 Maintenance Unit) ranged far and wide across Southern England collecting wrecked aeroplanes. Here, a Commer towing unit is pictured with a trailer load of wrecked Spitfire "somewhere in Sussex".

93. One wreck they had to deal with was this Junkers 88 at Croydon on 20th February 1944. Here they get to grips with collecting the pieces and taking them back to their Sussex base.

HORSHAM URBAN DISTRICT

In common with many areas in Sussex that day, Horsham was hit by an air attack on 10th February 1943, when bombs struck Wimblehurst Road, Richmond Road and Craven Lodge. In this attack there were three serious casualties and six slightly injured. Two houses were destroyed and over sixty damaged and it was certainly fortunate that nobody was killed. This proved to be the last air raid on Horsham for over a year.

In the intervening period, however, there were a number of aircraft incidents in the area - the first of these being a Tiger Moth which came to earth at Broadbridge Heath on 10th July 1943. The next incident involved the shooting down of a bomb-carrying Focke Wulf 190, also at Broadbridge Heath, on 21st November 1943. Hit by a Mosquito night fighter the German plane crashed and broke up at Wickhurst Lane after the pilot, Fw. Jorga, baled out and landed in Cobb's Wood, Billingshurst, where he was captured. The following morning he was taken to the place where his aeroplane had crashed, causing great excitement for the wide-eyed schoolboys scavenging there for souvenirs!

The next loss involved the collision of two Spitfires at 9,000 ft over Horsham on 6th December when practising tactics and formation flying. For no apparent reason one of the Spitfires flew into another in the formation and both fell from the sky. Fg. Off. Heninger baled out of his machine which crashed at Southolme, Roffey Corner, while the other Spitfire crashed outside the District killing the pilot.

The last air raid on the town took place on the 24th March 1944, when a number of incendiary bombs and one unexploded 250 kg bomb fell 30 yds west of the Horsham - Dorking railway line. No damage was caused but a speed limit of 5 mph had to be imposed on the railway until the UXB could be cleared.

Two days after D-Day, on 8th June, two bomb-laden RAF B-25 Mitchell bombers collided over the town and crashed to earth exploding at Amies Mill and Picts Hill. All eight Dutch Naval Air Service crewman of the Dunsfold based 320 Squadron were killed.

The V1 Flying Bomb campaign which started in June was, to a large extent, plotted via the Horsham based Operations Centre of 2 Group, Royal Observer Corps. Incoming bombs were plotted and tracked for the defenders and to also alert areas possibly affected on the bomb's route. To the ROC and RAF these weapons were "Divers", the code-name given to Flying Bombs. To the public they were more generally known as "Doodlebugs" or "Buzz Bombs" after the peculiarly unique vibrating roar the pulse jet motors made. For those on the ground a sigh of relief would result if any "Doodlebug" passed overhead - as that bomb would now be someone else's problem or worry! If, however, the motor stopped as it approached, there was deathly silence for about ten seconds before impact and explosion. They would surely be the longest ten seconds in the lives of countless Sussex residents.

On the ground at Horsham the residents knew only too well about the terror of the V1. The first experience of one was on 29th June, when a "Doodlebug" was shot down by RAF Fighters, shattering scores of windows and slates in West Street and Bishopric. There was a view that these bombs were targeted on London - and perhaps the RAF should leave well alone! Surely it would have been only too easy to have thought so if one had been standing in West Street on 29th June 1944! Other flying bombs exploded at Highlands Farm at Holmbush and near St. Leonards Forest House. Damage was caused but there were no fatalities.

The war was winding to its conclusion when a dramatic event struck Mannings Heath on 17th February 1945, with the crash and explosion of a Halifax bomber. Outbound to attack Wesel one of the engines caught fire and the pilot, Flt. Lt. T. N. Winning, ordered the crew to abandon the 51 Squadron Halifax. All escaped safely except Winning and the Bomb Aimer, F. Sgt. N. Baggs. Winning was found near the aeroplane, but Baggs had failed to exit the stricken bomber and died in the wreckage. The stark facts are fully detailed in the official reports of the time, but maybe it would be interesting to look at the incident through the eyes of an eye witness. Here then is the account of Don Bateman:

"As an eleven year old schoolboy I was on the

village green at Mannings Heath on a Saturday afternoon with my close pal, Peter Dawes, awaiting another lad who was joining us looking for golf balls at Mannings Heath Golf Course. These balls we traded in for bars of chocolate with Canadian Army Officers.

It was a typical winter afternoon, overcast and misty and at approximately 2 pm I heard the roar of aircraft engines, and saw a four engined Halifax bomber banking beyond the Mannings Golf Club Clubhouse, within seconds there was a violent explosion followed by a fireball. At this time we dived flat on our faces and must have stayed down for some time.

Within minutes people appeared from all directions and headed onto the golf course, us included.

As we ran down the first fairway a crew member was landing by parachute and RAF Auster spotter planes were encircling the scene, and subsequently landed on the eighteenth fairway. On arriving at the scene of the crash, which was in woodland down below the 16th green, it was clear little could be done as fires were raging and machine gun ammunition exploding. There was a large crater in the ground and pieces of aircraft strewn over a great area, full grown oak trees had been thrown like match sticks onto the second and third fairways. One of the landing wheels had been blown approximately a mile as the crow flies into the garden of "The Quarries" in Winterpit Lane and was standing in a vertical position against a rose pergola. It was discovered by my father who was employed on the estate next day.

Of the crew of seven, one went down with the plane and the pilot either baled out too late, or was caught in the blast, as I remember seeing his body with his parachute under an oak tree on the other side of the stream on the fourth. The remaining members of the crew baled out safely and, I understood at the time, one landed at Winterpick Farm".

This was the account of one young schoolboy for whom the war years had been times of high drama and excitement. The awful reality of war was far removed from the novelty of it all and yet children, as well as the adults, were affected by all the ghastly manifestations warfare. Young Don Bateman must have been profoundly affected by what he experienced and saw that day at Mannings Heath - but lived to tell the tale. On the other hand, two of the eight fatal civilian casualties in the Urban District were children. Nine year old Joan Hunt and six year old Audrey Sexton were evacuees from London who, ironically, had been sent to the "safety" of Horsham. In wartime Sussex, nowhere was safe.

94. Horsham remained home for the H.Q. of 2 Group, Royal Observer Corps throughout the war. Here, one of their volunteer Observers (motto " Forewarned is Forearmed ") watches and waits for incoming raiders or V1s at his post " ....somewhere in Sussex ."

95. Unusual was the Patriot Engineering Works, a Horsham based volunteer organisation which produced machined items for the war effort. The youngest volunteer was a 9 year old boy, Michael, who did his patriotic stint on the drills!

HOVE MUNICIPAL BOROUGH

Tragedy struck Hove during March 1943, when on the 9th a raiding force hit the Borough in a particularly fierce attack which left eleven dead and scores injured at Shelley Road, Aldringham Avenue and Walsinham Terrace. Still recoiling from this horror, a force of Focke Wulf 190's were back again on 29th March to further terrorise Hove. This time twelve civilians died as bombs rained down on Nizells Avenue, Shirley Street, New Church Road and Colbourne Road. Indirectly, it was probably these two lethal raids which then caused the loss of an RAF Mosquito on 2nd April.

Approaching Hove from the sea the twin engined aircraft could easily have been a German Junkers 88 when viewed head-on by nervous anti-aircraft gunners. An Air Raid Warning "Red" was in force at the time and Ground defence weapons put up a curtain of very accurate fire towards the Mosquito with the result that the plane was hit several times and crashed into a railway cutting between Hove and Portslade Stations. Moments before impact Squadron Leader Sutton, the pilot, baled out badly wounded but his observer, Pilot Officer Streeter, was killed - his body was later recovered from the burnt out wreckage. For three hours the railway line was blocked as rescuers moved the wreckage and investigators began an enquiry into this tragedy.

On 16th March 1944, an American Lightning crashed into the sea off Hove, its pilot rescued by launch and taken to Newhaven. Another USAAF aircrew were thankful for the services of the Newhaven Air Sea Rescue Launch on 23rd May when their B.17 Flying Fortress came down in the sea offshore from Hove. Nine of the crew were rescued on this occasion.

With the onset of the V1 Flying Bomb campaign Hove was fortunate in that not one fell in the Borough, although many passed overhead. One of these narrowly missed the windmill close to the ARP Control Centre but flew on to crash and explode harmlessly in open ground outside the Borough.

With the war drawing to a close in Europe unpleasant memories of the tragedy involving the Mosquito were awakened on 6th May, 1945, when another aircraft of this type crashed in poor visibility and burnt out at Dyke Road, killing Flt. Sgts D. P. Williams and K. Rhoden.

At the end of hostilities 24 civilians and 7 service personnel had been killed, 80 buildings totally destroyed and 3,875 damaged, 91 high explosive bombs had fallen, one parachute mine and 1,300 incendiaries. Although the residents of Hove did not have the satisfaction of seeing any of the raiders brought down within its boundaries, post war research has established that one of the attackers on 29th March 1943, was shot down off Brighton by a Spitfire of 610 Squadron. The aircraft, a Focke Wulf 190, sank in the sea and Uffz. J. Koch was killed.

96. This was the scene on 9th March 1943, after Hove's biggest air raid of the war.

97. The ten aircrew of a USAAF B-17 Flying Fortress prepare for another mission over Germany. On 23rd May 1944, a Fortress crew like this one had good cause to be thankful of the RAF Air Sea Rescue branch when they ditched in the sea off Hove.

LEWES MUNICIPAL BOROUGH

Little East Street, Brook Street, North Street, New Street, West Street, New Road and St. Martins Lane were all either hit or damaged in a sharp fighter bomber attack at around 12.40pm on Wednesday, 20th January 1943. Considering the widespread damage and time of day the casualties were surprisingly light. Nine year old Stanley Johnson was killed, and around 45 people injured in a raid which left the County Town of East Sussex battered and shaken. Canadian soldiers in the town, under the Command of Captain J. J. Mac. A.Sharpe, put in some sterling work salvaging materials and belongings from the bombed houses and in clearing up the debris.

Returning from operations over Europe a Halifax bomber approached the town from the south during the early evening of 17th April 1943, and was clearly in some difficulty. Moments later it had crashed into allotments on Landport Estate on the Offham Road and caught fire. Incredibly all eight occupants survived the crash although seven were injured and taken to the nearby Victoria Hospital. The eighth man, Flt. Lt. Wood (the pilot) was unhurt and the NFS, soon on the scene, quickly had the fire under control.

In May of the following year, on the 14th, a stray shell from an army firing practice range crashed into the same allotments and exploded - injuring a man who was working there. The same day stray shells killed two members of the Home Guard elsewhere in Sussex giving rise to questions in the House of Commons by Lewes MP, Rear Admiral T. P. H. Beamish. These incidents highlighted the dangers the civilian population were often unavoidably placed in by friend rather than by foe. In fact, the rain of shrapnel, spent bullets and cartridge cases from the sky could be positively lethal and many people were injured or killed in this way- particularly during the Flying Bomb period when the sky was filled with exploding ordnance of every kind. After all, everything that went up had to come down! During the Flying Bomb attacks only one of these weapons fell - in the south of the Borough - but caused no casualties and no significant damage.

As the end of the war approached an American Mustang fighter made it as far as Lewes on the 6th February 1945, before its petrol ran out on completion of a round trip to Germany where it had been escorting heavy American bombers. 1st. Lt. George Kemper baled out and landed near Ringmer, leaving his aeroplane to smash itself to pieces on the chalk Downs at Cliffe Hill, South-Malling-Without.

At the end of the war Lewes had experienced 1,051 air raid warnings, three civilians had been killed, thirty houses destroyed. Throughout all this the volunteers of the ARP organisation ran an exemplary service to the town and, in recognition, the Chief ARP Officer, Mr. C. G. Sains, was awarded the British Empire Medal. When the organisation stood down on 2nd May, just a week prior to VE-Day, it was with some justifiable pride that Lewes was able to boast its Civil Defence service had been composed entirely of volunteers with not one single "conscript" drafted to them under Compulsory Enrolment Orders as was the case in many other areas.

98. Snapped illicitly across allotments this private photograph shows the broken up fuselage and tail of the Halifax bomber at Landport on 17th April 1943. (Private photography of this kind was highly illegal!).

99. The volunteers of the Civil Defence force at Lewes on parade. Note the anti-blast tape on the windows of the house.

LITTLEHAMPTON URBAN DISTRICT

The first notable incident during 1943 was the loss of the Dutch cargo vessel, "S.S. Frode", blown up and sunk by a mine about four miles out to sea between Littlehampton and East Preston on 11th April. Three survivors, all badly burned and shocked, were brought ashore and treated at Littlehampton Hospital. They were Norwegians Hans Henderson and Rolf Buker, and a Royal Naval Gunner, Frederick Snape, who was manning anti - aircraft guns on board. The remainder of the crew were rescued and taken to Portsmouth and one dead member of the crew was also brought in at Littlehampton. Rolf Buker, the ships 2nd Engineer, died in Hospital on the 13th April.

The night bombers were back on the night of 15th/16th August when bombs were dumped in fields at the rear of Bellscroft Close and Southfields Road, Littlehampton. These bombs failed to disperse from their containers but ignited thirty stacks of cut oats and also set light to grassland. Many of the bombs did not ignite and were dealt with by bomb disposal experts the next day. Several of the small magnesium bombs were found to have explosive capsules in the tail - a type of bomb which was quite deadly and which, when it exploded, spread over a greater area the incendiary agent. In itself, this was an unremarkable episode but was typical of hundreds of such incidents throughout Sussex during the war.

Just prior to this incident a Lancaster bomber went into the sea off Littlehampton on 13th August - just opposite Norfolk Road. The bomber, from 619 Squadron, had collided with another Lancaster (see also Petworth Rural District) over the coast returning from Milan. With damage to the port wing the aeroplane was put into a tight diving turn in taking further avoiding action. Both outer engines caught fire in the dive, but the fire were later extinguished. Down to 1,000 ft the Lancaster then attempted to land at Shoreham but could not get down because another aircraft was on the runway. Flying out to sea, the Lancaster then flew down the coast losing height until it struck the sea and ditched off Littlehampton. The crew scrambled clear of the bomber and five of the seven made it into their rubber dinghy. One, the Navigator Sgt. Jones, drifted away and his body was recovered from the sea on 21st August. The rear gunner, Sgt. Maddaford, was picked up from the sea apparently drowned but after artificial respiration he showed signs of recovery. Sadly, he died in hospital later that same day. The survivors were collected by Air Sea Rescue launch, 45 minutes after going into the water.

The fatal loss of a Beaufighter which crashed at the rear of Parkside Estate on the 21st October claimed the lives of Fg. Off. R. L. Watts and Pt. Off. G. B. Thomas of the Fighter Interception Unit at nearby Ford. They had been mistakenly shot down by Canadian Anti - Aircraft Gunners.

On 18th June the unmistakable throb of an approaching V1 could be heard, and as anxious eyes peered seawards to spot the approaching unwelcome visitor the realisation dawned that it was coming from inland, flying north to south! Without fail, there weapons flew a direct and straight course towards London without deviation and were generally unable to bank or turn without crashing to earth. The report on this episode concludes: *"The bomb passed over Rustington and fell into the sea, exploding at map reference 480180, 2 miles from shore. No damage or casualties. The cause of the bomb falling, and the unusual course it was taking, was not ascertained".*

On lst August 1944, an aircraft escape hatch window fell at Surrey Street causing damage to the roof of T. Symer and Sons. According to the record there were no injuries on the ground and there was no indication as to where the window had come from. It is possible, however, that it fell from a Mustang fighter which crashed on this date at Michelgrove Farm, north-west of Poling. The 339 Fighter Group Pilot had baled out returning to England following a collision with another Mustang in the area of the battle lines.

On 17th February 1945, a tragic flying accident took the lives of two RAF aircrew and three civilians. Taking off from RAF Ford in his Mosquito, Wing Commander William Maguire, DFC (see also Eastbourne) experienced engine problems and could not avoid crashing into bungalows at Chaucer Avenue, Rustington, catching fire and demolishing four of the dwellings. Both he and his Navigator, Fg. Off. D. Lake, DFM, were killed instantly - as were Edward Vincent (63), Arthur Foster

(57) and Florence Ward (50). Mrs. Rockall and her young baby were also injured in the flaming debris and lucky to survive. This terrible accident was the last episode of any particular note in the Urban District before VE Day in May.

100. An unknown German airman is buried at Littlehampton during September, 1943. As was customary he is afforded full military honours by the Royal Air Force.

MIDHURST RURAL DISTRICT

The enemy raiders which attacked far and wide across Sussex on 10th February 1943, also struck Midhurst when a Dornier 217 released bombs which hit Sheepcote in Sheep Lane. Barbara Merrington (wife of Cpl. Walter Merrington, RAF), and her four year old son, Peter, were both killed, as was Florence Wheeler, another occupier of Sheepcote.

Retribution of a kind was exacted by the RAF upon the Luftwaffe Dornier 217 force during the night of 7th/8th March when one was shot down in flames by a Beaufighter at Vann Common, Fernhurst. The pilot and his navigator were badly wounded but managed to escape by parachute and were taken prisoner. Not so fortunate were the Radio Operator and Gunner who were both killed as bullets and cannon shells ripped into their cockpit.

At the time of the nightfighter interception the Dornier was preparing for a glide - attack on shipping at Southampton and, consequently, when the bomber finally crashed into Reekes Wood the full bomb load was still aboard. I was not until 1989, however, that the wreckage was finally uncovered and evidence found that bombs were still present. Consequently, an RAF Bomb Disposal Team was called in to investigate the site and duly recovered and rendered safe five 50kg bombs and two 500kg bombs in an operation lasting two weeks and which involved the discovery of the largest cache of German bombs in England post - war. During the operation to recover these bombs extensive excavations were conducted at the site and copious amounts of wreckage were unearthed. However, it was surprising that not a trace could be found of the Gunner, Gefreiter Franz Huske, who remains missing to this day. His comrade, Radio Operator Hans Witkopp, was found in 1943 amongst the wreckage and lies buried at Chichester.

Rather less dramatic were the crashes of RAF Tiger Moth aircraft on 19th March, 22nd September and 5th November at Wardley Hanger, Nyewood Post Office and Woodmans Hatch Green respectively.

On 4th October 1943, eighteen high explosive bombs were dropped on Bepton shortly after 11pm. Damage was caused at Upper House Farm, Manor Farm and Elsted Railway Station and eleven houses and farm buildings were damaged also. The only casualties were one horse and two cows killed, most of the bombs falling harmlessly in open country or woodland. No other episodes of note are recorded in the district for the remainder of 1943.

On 20th January 1944, the first Tempest fighter to crash was lost at Ambersham Common, Heyshott, whilst on a test flight prior to delivery to the RAF. Tempest JN 747 was a write - off, but its pilot escaped by parachute.

At Linchmere on 25th January a USAAF Lockheed Lightning crashed in a wood at Stanley's Farm and was burnt out after its pilot, Thomas Connel, abandoned the aeroplane by parachute. He was treated for minor injuries at the King Edward VII Sanatorium, Easebourne, although the pilots of two other Lightnings which fell in the district were both killed. The first of these was at Ball Wood, Bepton, on 8th June and the other at Fitzlea Farm, Graffham, on 4th July. In the Bepton incident a Special Constable and Fireman were both injured by exploding ammunition, but even in post war years ammunition from this crash was still proving hazardous when children were injured in the 1950s after tampering with live rounds. Children are also said to have been responsible for rolling one of the fighters engines down the steeply sloping side of the Downs at this site.

On 29th March 1944, ten unexploded British 500lb bombs fell at Chilgrove while a formation of aircraft was passing overhead and a 1,000lb bomb fell without exploding 25 feet from the main Chichester to Petersfield Road near Harting causing the road to be closed until 16th April when the bombs were made safe.

On 30th June 1944, two Lancaster aircraft of 15 and 514 Sqns out-bound for an attack on Occupied Europe collided over Cocking at 5,000 ft. One of the aeroplanes (514 Sqn) caught fire and exploded in mid-air, showering wreckage, bombs and bodies across a wide area of Bepton and onto Pitsham Common, Cocking. Five of the crew died, but two landed by parachute only slightly injured. The 15 Sqn Lancaster crashed at Ford.

On 9th February 1945, an Auster communications aircraft came down at Wispers, Stedham, and yet another Tiger Moth on 12th April - this time at Dumpford Manor Farm, Elsted.

With the war in Europe drawing to a close the last aircraft incident in the district was to be a Spitfire of 310 Squadron, lost on 2nd May. Flt Sgt. Kratochvil, a Czechoslovakian, force-landed with engine failure in a ploughed field at Upperfold Farm, Fernhurst. On landing, the Spitfire broke up, overturned and caught fire trapping the pilot under the wreckage. He was pulled clear by Mr.Humphrey of Upperfold Farm and later taken to hospital at Haslemere with head injuries and burns.

On the same day a twelve year old boy, Brian Mitchell, was severely injured by the explosion of a detonator with which he was tampering. The device had been picked up in an Army training area and the boy connected the detonator by wires to an electric light socket at Midhurst Grammar School whereupon the device exploded. Incidents of this nature were by no means unusual, and the Sussex area reports are littered with accounts of children tampering with explosive devices they had found - sometimes with tragic or fatal results. Although the war was at an end, explosives from those years continued to pose a threat to the unwary and foolhardy. Even after more than fifty years objects of this nature may still be found and are still very potent. This point was graphically illustrated with the discovery of German bombs at Fernhurst during 1989.

101. On 8th March 1943, a Dornier 217 was shot down at Fernhurst. Gunner Franz Huske was killed but his body never recovered.

102. **In 1989 an RAF Bomb Disposal team excavated the crash site to search for unexploded bombs believed to be in the wreckage.**

103. **This was part of the large haul of UXB's. Bomb disposal experts on site at Fernhurst listen for the clockwork time delay fuse ....**

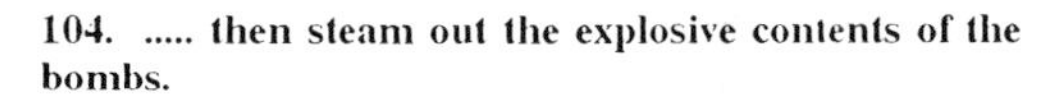

104. **..... then steam out the explosive contents of the bombs.**

NEWHAVEN URBAN DISTRICT

Newhaven's ordeal by bombing had, to all intents and purposes, ended in 1942 - there being no significant air raids on the port after that date and most of the town's eighteen civilian war dead had been killed in the earlier attacks of 1940. Nevertheless, the war was far from over!

The first aircraft loss in the period of this book seems to have been a Wellington of 29 Operational Training Unit down in the sea off Newhaven on 30th August 1943, and attended by the Newhaven based RAF High Speed Launches of the Air Sea Rescue Service. The Wellington was only one of the hundreds of crashes dealt with in the Channel by Newhaven based launches of the Marine Craft Unit in the duration of the Second World War.

The greatest period of activity was during 1944 which saw the port in heavy use during and after the D-Day landings of 6th June. Like most ports, its role in the overall operation was a key one and the disabling of any harbour installations could have had serious consequences and been extremely disruptive to the finely worked out plans. Thus, when the V1 Flying Bombs began to fall one week after the invasion these were concerns that these weapons could prove catastrophic to the organisation and mobility of men, machinery and stores then being funnelled through the South of England and fed onwards into Normandy. Nowhere more keenly was this felt than at locations like the port of Newhaven. In the event, however, there were only two flying bombs which actually exploded on the District. The first was at Denton on 6th July when 75 homes were damaged and the second was on 30th July when a low-flying V1 hit the cliffs and exploded near Newhaven Fort. It was the Flying Bomb incident on 12th July, however, which was the most alarming and the most tragic.

Approaching from Seaford, watchers on the ground observed a V1 with a Spitfire in hot pursuit and then, following a burst of gunfire, the "Doodlebug" exploded violently in mid air. Flying straight into the blast the Spitfire pilot, Fg. Off. George McKinley, lost control of his aeroplane (RB142 of 610 Squadron) which then dived to the ground at The Brooks, Drove Road, and burst into flames killing McKinley instantly. To the witnesses it seemed the young pilot had saved the town from the potential tragedy of a V1 exploding on it, and then sacrificed his own life by steering the crippled fighter away from a built up area. Impressed by his courage, the Town Clerk wrote to Mrs. McKinley telling her of the brave way in which her son had died.

On 25th August 1944, a British torpedo came close to causing havoc when it was accidentally fired by a ship in the harbour. The torpedo passed through a moored vessel and then settled on the bed of the harbour without detonating, later being retrieved by Newhaven Diver, Mr. Thomas Knight. In recognition of his brave work Mr. Knight was awarded the BEM. Then, at 5.00am on 22nd November, came the biggest explosion in the county during the entire war.

Loaded with 180 tons of a very high explosive a barge broke away from its tug during a storm, drifted ashore at Newhaven and washed up below the cliffs west of the town. Driven onto the beach the vessel struck a land mine and exploded with an extraordinary violence. The blast was felt as far away as Hailsham and heard way beyond. Closer to Newhaven, hundreds of windows were smashed in Lewes and Seaford, but in Newhaven almost every house was damaged with hardly a single roof or window intact. Many people were blown bodily out of bed and there were hundreds of minor injuries. Mercifully, there were only seven serious injuries and one fatality, a Naval rating killed when a wall fell on him. Had the explosion happened later in the day the casualty list and death toll would doubtless have been far higher. As it was, the cliff face also helped deflect the blast otherwise the effects could have been much worse in this the second largest wartime explosion in the whole country.

All things considered, Newhaven had had a lucky escape with its eighteen civilian war deaths. So easily could that figure have been increased to hundreds in that one incident alone. Sometimes the fortunes of war were of an almost benevolent disposition!

105. Leaving a foaming wake, RAF High Speed Launch 156 races down the Channel during 1943 on yet another rescue operation out of Newhaven. A 20 mm Oerlikon cannon on the stern provides anti-aircraft protection.

106. Having reached the scene of a reported crash the crew of HSL 156 find an RAF pilot in the water, still attached to his parachute. One of his rescuers prepares to throw the pilot a lifeline before bringing him back to Newhaven.

107. The great clear-up gets underway in Newhaven on 22nd November 1944, after the county's biggest explosion caused when 180 tons of high explosive detonated on the foreshore in a drifting barge. Damage was widespread and extensive, but only one person was killed.

PETWORTH RURAL DISTRICT

In 1943 Petworth was still reeling form the awfulness of the attack in September 1942, which had hit the Boys School and killed so many (See *Blitz Over Sussex 1941-42*). Such was the anxiety that this single raid had caused that the approach of any aircraft was viewed with consternation and the terminal screaming of a crippled aircraft overhead during the early morning of 13th August 1943, was alarming to say the least. Lancaster "R for Robert" was in its death dive having sustained critical damage in a collision with another Lancaster. All of the crew abandoned "Robert" with its over-revving engines and left it to dive to destruction at Plaistow where it fell on farmland without damage to property. Six of the crew landed safely but, despite a search, no trace could be found of the seventh man although it was known that he had baled out. It was not until March of 1944 that Sgt. Goodsall's body was discovered in Kingspark Wood, Plaistow.

At Fisher Street Farm, Northchapel, a Fleet Air Arm Fulmar crashed and was badly damaged on 19th August although Lt. J. Low and Air Gunner J. Cranch (the two occupants) were both uninjured. In crashing, the Fulmar brought down overhead power lines thus disrupting local electricity supplies.

Less dramatic was the crash landing of a Miles Magister trainer at Mill Farm, Shillinglee, on 8th April 1944. The record states, however, that damage was caused to a wheatfield, in respect of which "....RAF authorities settled for the sum of eighteen shillings". Hopefully, this generous sum adequately compensated for the swathe cut by the aeroplane propeller through the unripened wheat - although one would suspect that the damage to the aircraft would have cost considerably more than eighteen shillings to set right!.

Key Fox Farm, Petworth, was the scene of demise for an RAF Mustang on 25th June when it dived to earth killing its Air Transport Auxiliary pilot, 2nd Off. Thomas Fisk.

A Flying Bomb on 17th July caused tragedy when it fell on Diddisfold Cottage, Northchapel, killing nineteen year old Dorothy Mann and her son of two weeks - shown simply in the official records as Baby Mann.

One final fright was in store when, on 7th January 1945 a V2 Rocket exploded in mid-air at 05.30 hrs just across the Surrey border. Moments later fragments of metal debris were strewn across the Northchapel area but fortunately causing no damage or injury.

When VE Day finally came the joy and relief of the event for the people of Petworth was tempered with sadness and grief still felt for the Boys School tragedy - an event which had traumatised the town. More than fifty years later it is still a subject which many in Petworth find difficult or unable to discuss and which evokes powerful memories. Half a century has not eased all of the pain for all of those in Sussex who suffered.

108. On 13th August 1943, a Lancaster bomber like this one crashed at Plaistow after colliding with another Lancaster over the coast.

PORTSLADE URBAN DISTRICT

A daylight attack by Focke-Wulf 190 aircraft on 29th March 1943, left Ronald Akehurst, 33, of Brighton Civil Defence Service seriously injured. Admitted to the King Edward VII Sanatorium, Easebourne, Ronald finally succumbed to his wounds on 5th May. He was one of the unsung heroes of Civil Defence who regularly put themselves selflessly in mortal danger - men and women like this, just as much as our soldiers, sailors and airmen, were equally the defenders of this land and should never be forgotten.

Perhaps the most notable event in 1944 was the crash of a Douglas Havoc medium bomber during the late evening of D-Day, 6th June. The aeroplane came down at North House Farm Mile Oak, and was badly damaged although the three crew were uninjured. They were taken to Shoreham Airport and are identified in the records as "Lt. Charles C. Mish (Pilot), C.J. Clarke and R.F. Chustz" The wrecked aeroplane, number 310154, attracted a good deal of local interest on a day of intense excitement when over 11,000 aircraft had constantly roared across the skies of Southern England. To keep sightseers away the RAF Regiment from Shoreham mounted guard. There were no other incidents of significance in the District before victory in Europe was declared and the war was effectively at an end.

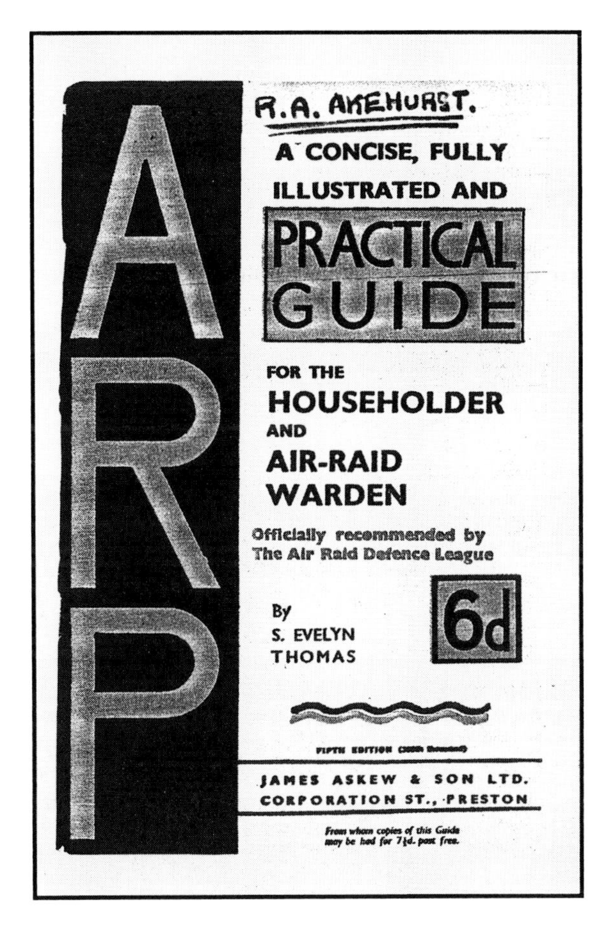

109. Ronald Arthur Akehurst of the Civil Defence Service was injured in an air attack on Portslade on 29th March 1943. He died at Easebourne Sanatorium on 5th May 1943. His ARP handbook was found in a 1990 clearance sale.

RYE MUNICIPAL BOROUGH

The raiders which had caused so much havoc and misery across the county on 10th February 1943, also visited Rye - causing deaths and damage to property at Havelock Villas. Gladys Axell, Matilda Barham and Eric Castle were all victims of this attack on the tiny Borough.

Fortunately, there were no other significant air raids on Rye - but the town was about to experience its most frightening ordeal when the Flying Bomb attacks started.

The biggest concentration of anti - aircraft artillery in the whole county was established to the south of Rye where no less than 1,300 gunners were encamped to combat the threat during the summer of 1944. When the barrage of weapons opened fire the cannonade was quite alarming in noise and intensity, and a rain of red hot shrapnel clattered down from the angry black puffs of exploding shells. From the ground it seemed that nothing could survive flying through such a fusillade of fire, and no less than six of these bombs were indeed brought down within the boundaries of Rye. It seems remarkable that only one loss of life resulted when farmer and Home Guardsman William Hacking was killed on 3rd July 1944, at his Cadborough Cliffe home.

No aircraft losses are recorded within the Borough during the 1943-45 period, but by the end of the war the civilian death toll stood at eleven. Fifty five houses had been destroyed and an astonishing 2,860 premises damaged - some of them more than once. On the other hand, no account of the part played by Rye in the overall war effort would be complete without mention of the £796,886 raised in the town through war savings. For such a small community it was an impressive sum which reflected the determined British spirit. The people of Rye may well have been battered, but they intended to show they were not beaten!

110. The sight and sound of the V1 "Doodlebug" struck fear into the population of Southern England. At Rye, six of these weapons fell within the tiny Borough.

SEAFORD URBAN DISTRICT

The air raids of 1941 and 1942 caused the last of the civilian deaths inthe District - although the remaining years of war were to be far from uneventful for the people of Seaford.

On 10th July 1943, during the early morning, a Halifax bomber ditched 100 yards off the Esplanade Hotel, Seaford, after being damaged by enemy action. The aeroplane was JD157 of 78 Squadron, the pilot of which ditched the bomber in a 3-point attitude before it settled into the waves and sank. All of the crew escaped, with the wireless operator swimming ashore while another four waded ashore. The sixth man on board, the rear gunner, was swept out to sea and picked up, semi-conscious, by an Air Sea Rescue Launch from Newhaven. Unfortunately, the aeroplane's dinghy release had failed to work because of battle damage and when the airmen finally managed its release it could not be inflated.

Further bombing occurred on 17th August 1943, when homes and a disused laundry in East Street were hit - but this was nothing in comparison to the attacks of 1941 and 1942 and there were only twelve minor casualties.

On 25th February 1944, there was an unhappy end to Warrant Officer H.S. McGill's attempts to force land his Typhoon on Seaford Head. Sadly, the aeroplane turned onto its back at the end of its landing run close to an Armoured Fighting Vehicle Range look - out post. Although official reports indicate the aeroplane was only slightly damaged Police Constable Frank Taylor found the young Australian pilot of 257 Squadron dead in his cockpit.

There was also a tragic end to the loss of a Spitfire of 317 Squadron on 18th May 1944, which crashed into Seaford Bay. Returning from a "Ranger" Operation to Dreux the young Polish pilot, Plt. Off. Mieczyslaw Adamek, was attempting to get back to his base at Deanland near Golden Cross when he was forced to abandon his ailing Spitfire, ML275. Unfortunately, he baled out too low for his parachute to open and was killed - his body later recovered by Minesweeper and brought ashore at Newhaven. In a sad footnote to the official report the following is recorded:
"Personal property on body:- 1/5d in silver and coppers. Comb in a case. 3 razor blades. 2 photos. 1 glove. 1 handkerchief. 1 FBD pack. 1 red neckerchief bearing the initial "A" and the word "Micky" and 7 embroidered swastikas."

"Micky" Adamek had clearly claimed seven enemy aircraft destroyed, embroidering each claim onto his scarf. Unfortunately, he had now become a victim himself. Who knows....perhaps some Luftwaffe pilot was already marking his aeroplane with another "kill" tally even as Adamek's body was being retrieved from the sea. In the flying bomb attacks which commenced in June, Seaford had a lucky escape with only one falling in the area. This was at Blatchington Golf Course on 20th July, causing some damage but no casualties. It was also at Blatchington, on 28th August, that a returning USAAF P-38 Lightning of the 479th Fighter Group crash landed after a fighter bomber attack against rail targets in Europe. The pilot was unharmed. The last aeroplane down in the area was at Chesterton School, Eastbourne Road, where an Auster communication aeroplane, number RT484, made a forced landing on the playing fields and became entangled in telephone wires causing damage to the wings and undercarriage.

Counting the cost, the town of Seaford found that 23 of its townsfolk had died and 100 had been injured. 28 properties were destroyed and over 2,000 damaged in 1,053 air raid alerts which had rained 147 high explosive and 10,000 incendiaries across the district. There were also four machine - gunning attacks and in one of these Mr. William Price Tomley, the Chief Air Raid Warden, had been killed on his way to the ARP Control Room. This was in 1942, and his replacement was Major R. G. Willis who held this post until 1945. The valuable and hazardous service these Wardens provided was certainly significant and praiseworthy. It was often a thankless and unpleasant job and one which lacked any glamour. In Seaford's hour of peril these men and women certainly did splendid work.

111. A Halifax bomber like this one made a dramatic ditching on the foreshore at Seaford on 10th July 1943.

112. The sturdy Typhoon. Despite its robustness it was not strong enough to save the life of W/O H.S. McGill, killed when his Typhoon overturned in a forced-landing at Seaford on 25th February 1944.

SHOREHAM-BY-SEA URBAN DISTRICT

The role of Shoreham aerodrome continued to be an important one housing the Walrus, Lysander and Spitfire aircraft of 277 (Air Sea Rescue) Squadron but, on 13th February 1943, the field was subject to a heavy incendiary attack when over 100 of these bombs fell - fortunately without causing major damage.

A quick glance at the aircraft loss tables at the rear of this book will show how important was the task of air sea rescue and it will be seen that a number of aircraft losses at sea also occurred off Shoreham itself. Many of these were attended by amphibian Walrus aircraft of 277 Squadron - including a ditched Stirling bomber down on 10th April.

This particular Stirling had been chased by enemy fighters and had then run short of petrol over the English Channel, eventually crashing into the sea 3 miles off Shoreham. The Wireless Operator radioed the Stirling's predicament and Spitfires were sent to escort the ailing bomber from the French coast whilst a Shoreham based Walrus was waiting for it to ditch. The bomber crew carried out a perfect dinghy drill and then awaited collection by the Walrus, although unfortunately the text-book operation had a slightly comic ending when the over-enthusiastic Walrus pilot taxied into the dinghy and tipped all the occupants into the water! Happily, everyone was eventually rescued without further mishap.

On 14th July, however, the High Speed Launches and Walrus aircraft of the RAF's Air Sea Rescue service were not needed when the pilot of an American P-47 Thunderbolt dropped into the sea east of the West Pier. Lt. De Genaro of the 78th Fighter Group baled out and landed close to the fishing vessel "Little Old Lady" which picked him up and put him ashore at Newhaven. The abandoned Thunderbolt meanwhile had headed westwards from Shoreham and finally went into the sea off Peacehaven.

The beaches at Shoreham continued to be dangerous places (see also *Blitz Over Sussex 1941-42*) with a series of accidents involving loss of life through land mine explosions. On 5th September 1943, Cpl. G. Dowson, RAF was killed when he trod on a land mine and this episode was followed on 18th October when L/Cpl. Garner and Cpl. Cooley of 12th Bomb Disposal Unit, RE, Preston Barracks, Brighton, were killed in a land mine explosion. Then, on 9th November, two more men from this same unit were killed in a similar incident on almost the exact same spot - this time L/Cpl Godley and Sapper Parkin losing their lives.

One of the last bombs in the area was dropped on 28th May 1944, when one high explosive bomb fell at New Barn, Shoreham, causing extensive damage to a farm building and injuring four people.

The last aircraft loss recorded in the vicinity was a Spitfire down in the sea off Shoreham Harbour on 21st April 1945, sending yet more aircraft debris to the sea bed for later generations of fishermen to snag their nets on!

When the war was officially over there was a post-script to Shoreham's story. On 12th May, four days after VE Day, two German Naval personnel came ashore in a rather sorry state and rowing a broken down cabin motor boat. Arthur Zeggel and Kurt Stubben, who had stolen the boat from La Rochelle on 7th May intending to defect, were unaware that as they miserably bobbed along the English Channel the war was actually ending! Somehow, this bizarre episode put a new meaning to those immortal words " For you, the war is over. " Fortunately, the war was over.

113. Ubiquitous and amphibious! The Walrus aircraft of 277 (Air Sea Rescue) Squadron at Shoreham saved the lives of many of aircrew down in the Channel.

SOUTHWICK URBAN DISTRICT

It was almost as if the war had passed Southwick by in the years 1943-45 and no significant air raid incidents or aircraft losses have been found as recorded there during that period. It was New Years Day 1943, however, that the massive bomb which had buried itself beneath the Parish Church (see *Blitz Over Sussex 1941-42*) was finally made safe and extracted. This two-year saga had surely been drama enough for any community!

On 30th August 1944, however, there was a tragedy on the foreshore near the Power Station when two men, Alfred Sherrard and Roland Holes, were killed in a landmine explosion as they spent their lunch break beachcombing. A third man, Ernest Hibling, was seriously injured.

At the wars end, however, it was recorded that six civilians had lost their lives in the Urban District and there had been considerable damage to property. No area of Sussex, however small, was untouched or unaffected by this war which had put all civilians in the Front Line.

UCKFIELD RURAL DISTRICT

The first air raid victim in the District during 1943 was on 17th January when 65 year old Olive Collins was killed at Jubilee Cottage, Blackboys, in an isolated incident. Fortunately, there were no further air raid fatalities in the Uckfield District during the remainder of 1943 - but there were to be several more in 1944 as a result of V1 incidents. There was also an attack by fighter bombers on 20th January when Maresfield Camp, Nutley, East Hoathly, Framfield and Piltdown all came under machine gun and cannon fire. At Isfield a railway engine was also hit and damaged in this raid.

The loss of a Typhoon aircraft through engine faults was by no means uncommon, and it will be seen that there were many such crashes in the county of Sussex. On 13th February, for instance, Sgt R. W. Hornall of No. 1 Sqn. was obliged to make an emergency landing in a Typhoon following engine problems. Coming down in difficult country at Woodgate Farm, Dane Hill, the fighter ended up with its starboard wing smashed off and against the boundary of Woodgate Farm kitchen garden. Sgt. Hornall was unhurt and telephoned Biggin Hill to notify them from the Orderly Room of the nearby 5th Canadian Armoured Division.

On 2nd March incendiaries fell at Nutley, setting light to a straw rick whilst on 25th March forty-four houses were damaged at Nutley by seven bombs which were dropped in the village - three of which failed to explode. At Duddleswell Manor, Duddleswell, Sir George Shackerley had a very narrow escape from bombs which fell there in the same air raid.

The Spring saw a amazing coincidence involving a Typhoon pilot, Flying Officer D.J. Green of 83 Group Support Unit. On 7th April he made a forced landing at Long Field, Moons Farm, Piltdown, following technical problems with his aeroplane. Green was only slightly hurt and the episode was dealt with and reported on by PC 183 Cuthbert Meads. In itself, a far from remarkable incident. In fact, one could say that this was a commonplace event for the period. What made it unusual, however, was that Green was back again one month later on 6th May when problems with another Typhoon forced him to crash land at Goldstrow Farm, Piltdown, close by the scene of his earlier mishap. PC Cuthbert Meads was again sent to deal with the incident and one can only speculate on their conversation. As they met "Not you again!" was surely the greeting the two must have had for each other!

Aircraft incidents continued to occur, and on 9th June Fg. Off. J. MacFarlane's Spitfire of 421 Squadron crashed at Hoth Wood, Rotherfield. At the Convent of Notre Dame, Hartfield, by the edge of Ashdown Forest, one of the straggling B-17 Fortresses returning from Stuttgart crashed on 6th September and was almost completely wrecked. Seven of the crew were unhurt, But Lt. Peel, Lt. Jones and S. Sgt. Harrington all received head and facial injuries and were admitted and detained at Queen Victoria Hospital, East Grinstead. Following this incident the Police became alarmed to discover that live ammunition had been distributed to children as souvenirs by troops guarding the wreckage, and were then kept busy tracking down all of these illicit and dangerous souvenirs from local school children!

On 5th October a Halifax of 35 Squadron, returning from bombing Frankfurt, crossed the coast on two engines and struggled as far as Mayfield before crashing at Sharnden Manor. Three of the crew were uninjured, but four had serious injuries and were admitted to hospital in Tunbridge Wells.

Another Typhoon was lost due to engine failure on 17th October when Fg. Off. Else of 182 Squadron had to abandon his aeroplane near Crowborough, leaving it to crash near the Wireless Station at Kings Standing on Ashdown Forest.

It was also engine problems which caused Flt. Sgt. E. Hampson to bale out of his Spitfire of 405 RSU over East Grinstead, the machine falling to earth at Hoopyard, Forest Row.

Into January 1944, and a B-26 Marauder of the USAAF's 386th Bomb Group was the first aircraft down, crashing at Springhead Farm, Blacknest, Crowborough on the 26th.

With the "Little Blitz" and renewal of German air attacks on London there followed the losses of four German aircraft in quick succession; a Junkers 188 at Framfield on 23rd February, a Messerschmitt 410 at Halland on the same date, a Junkers 188 at Withyham on 24th February and a Heinkel 177 at Hammerwood on 2nd March. All four incidents were at night and were a considerable boost for local civilians and military personnel who had become only too accustomed to the increasing Allied air losses. However macabre the circumstances surrounding such German crashes they unquestionably provided a boost to morale! However, a parachute mine explosion at Cousley Wood, Wadhurst, on 28th February damaged a large number of houses and caused one serious and two minor casualties.

A Polish pilot, Flt. Lt. Jozef Marszalek, was killed when he crashed in his 303 Squadron Spitfire, EE625, at Funnels Farm, Nutley, on 16th May and this was followed by the loss of another Typhoon near Mark Cross, when Flt. Sgt. J. Alston spun into the ground and was killed on 9th June.

The first V1 Flying Bomb exploded on 17th June just 75 yards from Possingworth Park Hotel, causing extensive damage and sixteen people were injured. There followed another 146 V1s down in the Uckfield Rural District. These claimed three civilian lives; at Mayfield on 12th July, Withyham on the 18th and Crowborough on the 22nd. The worst loss of life through the explosion of a V1 in Sussex was at Crowborough Golf Course where a " Doodlebug ", shot down by a fighter, hit a Canadian army encampment on 5th July, killing eight soldiers and wounding seventeen.

At Tidebrook, near Wadhurst, the Church School was wrecked by a V1 shot down by a fighter and which exploded 25 yards from the schoolhouse. By some miracle there were no casualties, as all the older children had taken cover in an Anderson Shelter and the younger ones who were in the playground were hustled into a dug-out shelter. A plaque in the local church records deliverance from what could have been an awful tragedy on the scale of the Petworth School Incident (see *Blitz Over Sussex 1941-42*). It reads:- " *With thanksgiving to God for the preservation of the teachers and the scholars of Tidebrook Church School on 4th August 1944, when an enemy flying bomb shattered the school buildings. Honour and discipline* ". (In fact, the date is incorrectly carved as the 4th, although it was the 3rd).

By coincidence on 11th August the last V1 down in the district also fell at Possingworth Park Hotel where further damage resulted.

Losses of a Lancaster occurred at Rotherfield on 22nd June and another B-26 Marauder on 12th July at Forest Row. On the 26th at Ridgewood, Uckfield, little remained of Belgian Flt. Lt. "Gin" Seghers or his 91 Squadron Spitfire after a collision in mid air with a V1 The resulting explosion and fireball seemingly left only tiny pieces of confetti-like debris falling to earth.

On 14th September 1944, a massive explosion rocked the Rotherfield and Crowborough areas as a V2 rocket blew up in mid air above Rumsden Farm, Crowborough. This was the first V2 in Sussex, and only the thirteenth in the UK. The disintegrated and scattered parts proved to be of value to British Intelligence services seeking to discover the secrets and inner workings of these fearsome devices. The second V2 was on 28th January 1945, and this also exploded in mid air - this time above Carsison Wood, Forest Row. There were no casualties or serious damage to property in either incident, although the death dealing and destructive potential of these rockets was enormous.

With the " shooting war " in the UK all but over there was an unfortunate mishap at Horsegrove Farm, New Road, Rotherfield involving a Tiger Moth on 9th February 1945. The 567 Sqn. aeroplane had already made a forced-landing but then crashed on attempting to take off again and resulted in Flt. Sgt. Powell being injured.

The last recorded aeroplane crash was at Colemans Hatch, Hartfield, on 21st March when a Photographic Recognisance Unit Spitfire came down, piloted by Fg. Off. F. Adlam.

When it was all over, civilian fatalities stood at 21, and 174 had been injured. 34 houses had been destroyed and 3,044 damaged in a total of 723 "incidents".

114. On 30th May 1943, Oblt Alfred Stanke (2nd left) and his crew were shot down over Barcombe in a Junkers 88 and taken prisoner.

115. The adversary of Alfred Stanke and his crew on 30th May was Flt. Lt. J.P.M. Lintott, pilot of a nightfighter Mosquito who was later killed chasing another night raider on 9th July 1943.

116. The wrecked Junkers 188 down at Hale Farm, Withyham, on 24th February, 1944. Two crew were taken prisoner, the other two were killed. (Note the strange camouflage pattern).

117. Police officers pose with the swastika bedecked tailfin of the Heinkel 177 at Hammerwood on 2nd March 1944.

118. V2 Rockets are prepared for launch .... target England!. Four fell in Sussex, two of them in Uckfield Rural District area.

WORTHING MUNICIPAL BOROUGH

Worthing's first raid of 1943 took place on 8th February when Sugden Road, Homefield Road, and Lyndhurst Road all took direct hits. A total of nine people were killed and there were a considerable number of other casualties. Another raid was to hit the town one month later when bombs fell on Pembroke Avenue, Harvey Road and Grove Road, killing another nine victims. Meanwhile, the tally of aircraft lost offshore continued to rise.

On 27th March one of the night raiders was sent flaming into the sea off Worthing Pier with the loss of all four crew who had fallen victim to a patrolling Beaufighter.

July of that year opened with the crash of a Tiger Moth of 602 Squadron at Dancton Lane when the pilot, Flt. Sgt. Bagget, and his passenger were injured. According to local reports the incident also resulted in damage to one electricity pylon.

On 24th October there was an unusual loss when a Cierva Autogiro, flown by Flt. Lt. T. V. Welsh of 529 Squadron, came down into the sea 300 yards off the beach opposite King George V Avenue. This strange aeroplane was engaged on radar calibration flights, and at the time of its loss was doubtless working in calibrating the GCI Radar site at Durrington (See *Blitz Over Sussex 1941-42*). Flt. Lt. Welsh was rescued by a Walrus Air Sea Rescue aircraft and the Autogiro later towed ashore to safety.

The Autogiro was one of many aeroplanes which were lost in the Channel immediately off Worthing and aircraft wreckage was often being washed ashore during the war years. In fact, there is a record that on 19th October an aeroplane undercarriage and wheel from a bomber plane were found on the beach at Goring-on-Sea. It is, of course, impossible to say with any certainty where this originated - but it is quite likely that it came from the Junkers 88 lost on 27th March.

More aeroplane wreckage was washed ashore on 23rd and 29th January 1944, which included an empty German aircraft dinghy and parts of a fuselage - also German. The bodies of Uffz Hollman and Gefr. Anskat were also found on a nearby beach and it is established that these men died on 22nd January. It is said they baled out of a bomber which had been hit and damaged, but which subsequently made it back to France. However, the discovery of aircraft wreckage would throw some doubt on this. Surely there must be a connection between the bodies, the dinghy and the aeroplane parts?

Bombs again hit Worthing on 14th March 1944, with one 250 Kg bomb falling near Downlands Garage and another in the sports field by the waterworks at one minute past midnight. Both bombs exploded, causing damage to 100 houses, the Waterworks and to greenhouses at nearby Lyon Farm Nurseries. The raider also fired incendiary bullets indiscriminately across the town and a large furniture depository was destroyed by fire. Fortunately, there were no casualties.

Another bomb was delivered on the night of 28th May when a 500 Kg device exploded 200 yards north-east of Goring Gasholder and 400 yards South of the radar site at Durrington, causing damage to telephone wires and a sewer but no casualties. Had the bomb fallen a few hundred yards in either direction the potential for serious damage is plainly evident.

As preparations for D-Day quickened their pace there was understandable consternation about a Despatch Rider missing from the RAF Station at Durrington on 4th June. He had left at 15.30 hours to proceed to RAF Chailey and the report states that: "LAC Stoner, 1634977, must be found at all costs. All Districts informed". Unfortunately, the records leave us none the wiser about the outcome. However, with all leave cancelled in the run up to invasion it is more than likely that Stoner simply did a bunk and went AWOL to see his wife or girlfriend! In all probability there was nothing more sinister to it than that, but the high level of security meant that incidents of this nature had to be taken very seriously.

D-Day came and went in Worthing with the same level of excitement experienced all over Sussex and along the South Coast but an apparently innocuous discovery of a carrier pigeon at Sackville Road, Worthing, on 15th June, was treated with great urgency and the bird and its message were sent immediately to Wing House, London, the HQ of the Carrier Pigeon Service. Although their part in the war is infrequently mentioned there are numerous reports of such birds being found in Sussex, carrying intriguing coded messages.

The last episode of any note in Worthing during the period 1943-45 was the tragic loss of a Lancaster bomber of 49 Squadron on 17th December 1944. This aircraft crashed into the sea to the west of Worthing Pier and exploded with great violence as the bomb load detonated. The aeroplane had been seen in difficulties over the town at around quarter-to-six when outbound for an attack on Munich and it was felt locally that the pilot was struggling to control the Lancaster in order to clear the town before disaster finally struck. When the bomb load and petrol tanks exploded the shock wave damaged 140 shops and 233 dwelling houses, hotels, etc., to the extent that it was very clear how serious the damage would have been had it crashed into Worthing. All seven crew perished, but the only body found was that of Sgt. G. F. Callon, the rear gunner. Of the others there was simply no trace apart from four opened parachutes and the bloodstained battledress tunic of Sgt. H. Varey the Flight Engineer, discovered washed ashore at Onslow Court.

So easily could the loss of the Lancaster have resulted in a major disaster with massive civilian deaths. One can only speculate as to whether the actions of the pilot, Fg. Off. E G. Essenhigh, saved the town from a higher over-all death toll than the Borough total of fifty five dead which is where the figure stood at VE Day.

119. One of these peculiar looking Autogiro aircraft came down into the sea off Worthing on 24th October 1943. Its pilot was saved.

120. This seven man crew of a Lancaster bomber have successfully returned from a raid over Germany. On 17th December 1944, the seven crew of a Lancaster were killed when it crashed and blew up on Worthing beach, outbound for a raid on Germany.

WORTHING RURAL DISTRICT

Remarkably, the Civilian War dead toll in the Worthing Rural District was only seven, all of them during 1940 and 1941. However, air raid activity continued into 1943 and 1944 - albeit with fairly minimal and non-fatal results. Aircraft losses, however, continued to occur although all of those recorded during 1943 and 1944 were British or American.

On the 17th June 1943, a Typhoon of 182 Squadron suffered engine failure and its pilot, Warrant Officer D. K. Lovell, executed a forced landing at Findon. The next episode involved an American B-26 Marauder which made a forced landing at Holmbush Farm, Kingston-by-Sea, returning damaged from an operational flight with two of its seven crew injured.

On 30th September 1943, six members of a bomb disposal squad (1 officer 2 NCOs and 3 other ranks) were all killed in an explosion whilst they cleared minefields at Angmering.

At Lyminster, on 21st November, a Mosquito of 418 Squadron overshot on a single-engined landing at Ford and crashed near Lyminster Church killing Fg. Off. T. Thomson and Fg. Off. H. Skellenberg and this was followed by the loss of a Whitley bomber, number BD259, at Southern Olympic Field, Lancing, during the early hours of 30th November 1943. The crew of six Sgts were all uninjured and were escorted to Shoreham Police Station before returning to their unit at Tilstock, Shropshire.

Another Mosquito loss is recorded at Priors Leas, Poling, on 31st January 1944, resulting in the deaths of Fg. Off. Jones and Flt. Sgt. Settle. In this episode one of the four 500lb bombs on board could not be found and presumably remains unaccounted for to this day. Yet another Mosquito went down on 6th March with the loss of HK464 200 yards east of Sea Lane, Ferring.

Just prior to this, on 2nd March, a bombing episode affected the parish of Lancing with high explosive and incendiary bombs at Wellan Park, West End Way and Curds Nurseries. A number of properties were damaged but there were no casualties. There were casualties, however, during a rather more serious attack on Lancing on 14th March when 45 and 46 Monks Close took direct hits and were demolished. Six people were trapped but later released, although a total of twelve people were injured, one seriously. A total of 154 houses were damaged as well as four food shops and numerous greenhouses on Youngs Nurseries.

Two Spitfire losses followed on 7th May and 3rd August - both of them belly landings. The first was at Central Avenue, Findon, the other at Coombes. Both pilots were uninjured.

In the final days of the war the last aircraft down in the district was a Fairey Albacore which landed on the Downs north of Worthing on 25th April 1945, after engine failure. The aeroplane was en-route from Manston to Thorney Island when it was forced to put down. The crew of Fg. Off. Gadzos, W/O Joyce and L/A Simmonds were all uninjured. And so ended the war for the Worthing Rural District. In common with everywhere else it had been a period of drama, excitement, destruction and of sadness.

AIRCRAFT LOSS TABLES

ARUNDEL MUNICIPAL BOROUGH

1943

10. 2.1943	BEAUFIGHTER	ARUNDEL PARK	

1944

16. 3.1944	TYPHOON	ARUN RIVER BANK (A79)	
22. 6.1944	LIBERATOR B24	PARK FARM (A77)	
25. 9.1944	HORNET MOTH	ARUNDEL PARK	

1945 NIL

BATTLE RURAL DISTRICT

1943

4. 1.1943	DORNIER 217	FAIRLIGHT	
4. 1.1943	FOCKE WULF 190	CASTLE FARM, RYE	(D1)
15. 1.1943	FOCKE WULF 190	WINCHELSEA BEACH	
17. 1.1943	BEAUFIGHTER	WESTFIELD	
21. 2.1943	TIGER MOTH	CATSFIELD	
27. 2.1943	TIGER MOTH	ASHBURNHAM	
13. 3.1943	SPITFIRE	WINCHELSEA HALT	(D20)
26. 3.1943	SPITFIRE	GREAT SHOESMITH FARM, WADHURST	
10. 5.1943	TIGER MOTH	NINFIELD	
1. 7.1943	SPITFIRE	WINCHELSEA BEACH	
23. 7.1943	AUSTER	CATSFIELD	
25. 8.1943	TIGER MOTH	SEDLESCOMBE	
29. 8.1943	MUSTANG	MARLEY LANE, BATTLE	
6. 9.1943	FORTRESS B17	PETT LEVEL	(D19)
6. 9.1943	FORTRESS B17	IN THE SEA OFF PETT LEVEL	
6. 9.1943	VENTURA	PEASMARSH	(D10)
7. 9.1943	MUSTANG	CALBEC HILL, BATTLE	
18.10.1943	FORTRESS B17	ICKLESHAM	
20.12.1943	MESSERSCHMITT 410	PLAYDEN, RYE	(D17)

1944

2. 1.1944	FOCKE WULF 190	CAMBER SANDS, RYE	
30. 1.1944	SPITFIRE	TELHAM LANE, BATTLE	(D21)
5. 2.1944	FORTRESS B17	HURST GREEN	
15. 3.1944	TYPHOON	BREDE VALLEY	(D4)
19. 3.1944	BOSTON	LIDHAM HILL, BATTLE	
22. 3.1944	SPITFIRE	SEDLESCOMBE	
21. 4.1944	SPITFIRE	TICEHURST	
1. 5.1944	MUSTANG	BREDE MARSHES	
18. 5.1944	SPITFIRE	ETCHINGHAM	
22. 5.1944	SPITFIRE	SEDLESCOMBE	(D22)
22. 5.1944	SPITFIRE	MOUNTFIELD	(D23)
24. 5.1944	TYPHOON	ICKLESHAM	(D14)
27. 5.1944	SPITFIRE	ICKLESHAM	(D24)
6. 6.1944	MARAUDER B26	WHATLINGTON	
6. 6.1944	MARAUDER B26	ASHBURNHAM	
7. 6.1944	MARAUDER B26	EAST GULDEFORD, RYE	
10. 6.1944	MUSTANG P51	BECKLEY	
24. 6.1944	LIBERATOR B24	EAST GULDEFORD, RYE	
28. 6.1944	TEMPEST	EAST GULDEFORD, RYE	
1. 7.1944	TEMPEST	WINCHELSEA	(D2)
1. 7.1944	TEMPEST	PARKDALE, BATTLE	(D15)
3. 7.1944	TEMPEST	PLAYDEN, RYE	(D8)
5. 7.1944	TEMPEST	NETHERFIELD	(D11)
8. 7.1944	SPITFIRE	CATSFIELD	(D25)
11. 7.1944	MUSTANG P51	TICEHURST	
16. 7.1944	THUNDERBOLT P47	IDEN LOCK, RYE (D9)	
18. 7.1944	MOSQUITO	ETCHINGHAM	
23. 7.1944	THUNDERBOLT P47	BATTLE (Collided with aircraft below)	(D6)
23. 7.1944	THUNDERBOLT P47	SEDLESCOMBE	(D5)
31. 7.1944	TEMPEST	HOOE	
6. 8.1944	TEMPEST	NINFIELD	
9. 8.1944	TEMPEST	BATTLE	(D16)
21. 9.1944	VENTURA	EAST GULDEFORD, RYE	
24.10.1944	PIPER CUBS (4)	WADHURST	
24.10.1944	PIPER CUB	RYE	
1.11.1944	LANCASTER	HURST GREEN	

1945

6. 2.1945	AVRO ANSON	LOWER MARSHAM, PETT	(D3)
28. 3.1945	FORTRESS B17	RYE HARBOUR	(D18)
6. 4.1945	MUSTANG P51	SEDLESCOMBE	(D7)

BEXHILL MUNICIPAL BOROUGH

1943

30. 6.1943	SPITFIRE	NINFIELD ROAD	
6. 9.1943	FORTRESS B17	IN THE SEA OFF BEXHILL	
14.12.1943	SPITFIRE	CONSTABLES FARM, BEXHILL	
30.12.1943	LIBERATOR B24	IN THE SEA OFF BEXHILL	

1944

31. 7.1944	SPITFIRE	SANDHURST LANE, BEXHILL	
31. 8.1944	LANCASTER	BARNHORN, BEXHILL	
6.12.1944	PIPER CUB	CHARTERS TOWERS, BEXHILL	

1945 NIL

BOGNOR REGIS URBAN DISTRICT

1943

14. 3.1943	SPITFIRE	IN THE SEA OFF BOGNOR	
22. 4.1943	TYPHOON	BEATTY ROAD	(A 66)
30.11.1943	MOSQUITO	OFF SHORE AT FELPHAM	

1944

9. 2.1944	MUSTANG P51	IN THE SEA OFF BOGNOR	
24. 2.1944	HEINKEL 177	IN THE SEA OFF BOGNOR	
8. 6.1944	SPITFIRE	CHESSELS FARM FLANSHAM	
4. 7.1944	FORTRESS B17	FELPHAM	(A 76)

1945 NIL

BRIGHTON COUNTY BOROUGH

1943

7. 5.1943	TYPHOON	GRAHAM AVENUE	

1944

2. 2.1944	TYPHOON	EAST BRIGHTON	
8. 2.1944	FORTRESS B17	LONDON ROAD, BRIGHTON	
19. 4.1944	MESSERSCHMITT 410	DYKE ROAD	
26.11.1944	TYPHOON	BRIGHTON BEACH	(B26)

1945 NIL

BURGESS HILL URBAN DISTRICT

1943 NIL

1944

12. 7.1944	SPITFIRE	KEYMER ROAD	(B29)

1945 NIL

CHAILEY RURAL DISTRICT

1943

10. 2.1943	DORNIER 217	TELSCOMBE	(C49)
14. 3.1943	TYPHOON	TARRING NEVILLE	(C30)
16. 3.1943	SPITFIRE	IFORD	
16. 3.1943	THUNDERBOLT P47	NEAR LEWE	
18. 3.1943	SPITFIRE	DITCHLING	
27. 3.1943	MUSTANG P51	CLAYTON WINDMILL	
24. 4.1943	MOSQUITO	HOUNDEAN FARM, FALMER	
20.10.1943	FORTRESS B17	BEDDINGHAM	(C46)

1944

6. 2.1944	MOSQUITO	BEDDINGHAM HILL	
21. 2.1944	AUSTER	SOUTH HEIGHTON	
13. 5.1944	TYPHOON	BLACK CAP HILL	(C31)
8. 6.1944	LIGHTNING P38	TOY FARM, BEDDINGHAM	(C47)
11. 6.1944	SPITFIRE	WESTMESTON	
30. 6.1944	THUNDERBOLT P47	CHAILEY	
3. 8.1944	FORTRESS B17	PLUMPTON	
18.10.1944	LYSANDER	ADES FARM, CHAILEY	
9.11.1944	HALIFAX	GREAT HOME WOOD, CHAILEY	
19.11.1944	DAKOTA DC3	THE PLANTATION, FALMER	

1945 NIL

CHANCTONBURY RURAL DISTRICT

1943

21. 9.1943	MUSTANG P51	AMBERLEY	
2.11.1943	SPITFIRE	PULBOROUGH	

1944

26. 1.1944	OXFORD	WEST CHILTINGTON	
1. 4.1944	SPITFIRE	PARHAM	
26. 4.1944	SPITFIRE	STEYNING	
26. 4.1944	SPITFIRE	WASHINGTON	(B51)
2. 5.1944	SPITFIRE	SULLINGTON	
30. 5.1944	SPITFIRE	UPPER BEEDING	(B52)
11. 6.1944	SPITFIRE	SULLINGTON	
25. 6.1944	MOSQUITO	RED BARN, BEEDING	(B55)
4. 7.1944	FORTRESS B17	UPPER BEEDING	(B65)
1. 8.1944	TIGER MOTH	BEEDING MISSION HALL	

1945

6. 2.1945	FORTRESS B17	TRULEIGH HILL	(B63)
29. 3.1945	SPITFIRE	UPPER BEEDING	(B53)

CHICHESTER MUNICIPAL BOROUGH

1943 NIL

1944

11. 5.1944	LIBERATOR B24	THE HORNET, CHICHESTER	
13. 7.1944	SPITFIRE	GRAYLINGWELL HOSPITAL, CHICHESTER	(A89)

1945 NIL

CHICHESTER RURAL DISTRICT

1943

12. 1.1943	LIBERATOR B24	THORNEY ISLAND	
25. 1.1943	TIGER MOTH	FUNTINGTON	
4. 2.1943	HALIFAX	TANGMERE AIRFIELD	
10. 2.1943	DORNIER 217	LAGNESS	(A72)
19. 2.1943	BEAUFIGHTER	FORD	
1. 3.1943	TYPHOON	SIDLESHAM	(A67)
23. 3.1943	HAMPDEN	MARSHES, THORNEY ISLAND	
3. 4.1943	HAMPDEN	MARSH FARM, BINSTED (A71)	
9. 4.1943	HAMPDEN	WEST ASHLING	
15. 4.1943	WELLINGTON	SOUTH MUNDHAM	
16. 4.1943	TYPHOON	SELSEY GOLF COURSE	(A68)
18. 4.1943	TYPHOON	TANGMERE	
24. 4.1943	HAMPDEN	LIDSEY	
3. 5.1943	TYPHOON	OVING MANOR	
13. 5.1943	TYPHOON	ARUNDEL RAIL LINE	(A78)
12. 6.1943	MOSQUITO	NEAR FORD AIRFIELD	
19. 6.1943	TYPHOON	PAGHAM HARBOUR	
20. 6.1943	SPITFIRE	APPLEDRAM	
30. 6.1943	MUSTANG P51	FORD CHURCH	
23. 7.1943	HALIFAX	TANGMERE AERODROME	
11. 8.1943	HALIFAX	SELSEY BEACH	
23. 8.1943	TYPHOON	LAVANT	
10. 9.1943	MESSERSCHMITT 108	FORD AIRFIELD	
26. 9.1943	THUNDERBOLT P47	APPLEDRAM	
8.10.1943	WHIRLWIND	NORTHBARN FARM	(A70)
15.10.1943	TYPHOON	SHRIPNEY	
16.10.1943	TYPHOON	HAMBROOK	
20.10.1943	TYPHOON	NEAR ARUNDEL	
23.10.1943	MOSQUITO	COLEWORTH FARM BOGNOR	
6.11.1943	MOSQUITO	NEAR FORD	
11.11.1943	TYPHOON	MERSTON AIRFIELD	
19.11.1943	STIRLING	ARUN RIVER BANK	
19.11.1943	HALIFAX	NEAR FORD	
20.11.1943	TYPHOON	FONTWELL	
20.11.1943	HALIFAX	HANGER AT TANGMERE	
24.11.1943	SPITFIRE	YAPTON	(A88)
17.12.1943	LYSANDER	OVING	
17.12.1943	LYSANDER	FORD	
18.12.1943	TYPHOON	BOW HILL, CHILGROVE	

1944

5. 1.1944	SPITFIRE	CLIMPING	
18. 1.1944	WARWICK	PATCHING	
23. 1.1944	SPITFIRE	IN THE SEA OFF PAGHAM	
30. 1.1944	MOSQUITO	BILSHAM CORNER, YAPTON	
3. 2.1944	TYPHOON	IN THE SEA OFF SELSEY	
8. 2.1944	WELLINGTON	WAKEFORDS FARM, CHIDHAM	
8. 2.1944	MOSQUITO	WESTBOURNE	
11. 2.1944	MOSQUITO	WALBERTON	
13. 2.1944	LANCASTER	DUNCTON	
28. 2.1944	MOSQUITO	SOUTH MUNDHAM	(A69)
1. 3.1944	TYPHOON	WEST HARTING	
14. 3.1944	TYPHOON	ALDINGBOURNE	
24. 3.1944	JUNKERS 188	WALBERTON	(A73)
25. 3.1944	HALIFAX	CLIMPING ROAD, FORD	
3. 4.1944	SPITFIRE	EAST LAVINGTON	
8. 4.1944	HALIFAX	IN THE SEA OFF MIDDLETON	
8. 4.1944	HALIFAX	TANGMERE AERODROME	
9. 4.1944	ALBACORE	BRINKMANS NURSERY BOSHAM	
18. 4.1944	SPITFIRE	HOES FARM, SHIPLEY	
19. 4.1944	SPITFIRE	WEST DEAN	
25. 4.1944	AUSTER	ALDINGBOURNE	
18. 5.1944	SPITFIRE	FUNTINGTON	
20. 5.1944	THUNDERBOLT P47	SHRIPNEY	(A75)
21. 5.1944	SPITFIRE	CROCKER HILL, ARUNDEL	(A87)
23. 5.1944	FORTRESS B17	FORD AERODROME	
7. 6.1944	MUSTANG P51	MERSTON	
9. 6.1944	SPITFIRE	BINSTED	(A86)
9. 6.1944	MOSQUITO	FORD AERODROME	
14. 6.1944	MUSTANG P51	RATHAM FARM, FUNTINGTON	
18. 6.1944	TYPHOON	PRINSTED	
22. 6.1944	MARAUDER B26	YAPTON	
23. 6.1944	MOSQUITO	THORNEY ISLAND	
30. 6.1944	LANCASTER	FORD AERODROME	
17. 7.1944	SPITFIRE	WEST STOKE, FUNTINGTON	(A85)
18. 7.1944	SPITFIRE	BILSHAM FARM, YAPTON	(A84)
18. 7.1944	SPITFIRE	HAMMER FARM, SHIPLEY	
23. 7.1944	AUSTER	THE SLIPS, STOUGHTON	
1. 8.1944	MOSQUITO	FORD AERODROME	
7. 8.1944	FORTRESS B17	CLIMPING	(A74)
14. 8.1944	MOSQUITO	FORD AERODROME	
29. 8.1944	SPITFIRE	IN THE SEA OFF SELSEY BILL	
9. 9.1944	MOSQUITO	THORNEY ISLAND AIRFIELD	
10. 9.1944	SPITFIRE	NEAR WESTHAMPNETT	
11. 9.1944	TYPHOON	BERSTED	(A80)
22.10.1944	MOSQUITO	FORD AERODROME	
21.11.1944	SPITFIRE	DRAYTON	(A83)
19.12.1944	HALIFAX	FORD AIRFIELD	

1945

28. 1.1945	FAIREY	SWORDFISH WEST STRAND, WITTERING	
10. 2.1945	LANCASTER	THORNEY ISLAND	
11. 2.1945	DAKOTA DC3	UPWALTHAM DOWN	
22. 2.1945	SPITFIRE	SUNT COTTAGES, SHIPLEY	
13. 3.1945	SPITFIRE	OAK FARM, TANGMERE	

CUCKFIELD RURAL DISTRICT

1943

6. 2.1943	MUSTANG P51	PYECOMBE	(B27)
12. 3.1943	HALIFAX	HANDCROSS	
16. 3.1943	SPITFIRE	BISHOPSTONE FARM, CUCKFIELD	
10. 7.1943	HALIFAX	STAPLEFIELD	

1944

2. 7.1944	PIPER CUB	POYNINGS	
17.10.1944	DAKOTA DC3	FULKING	
25.12.1944	AVRO ANSON	BOLNEY	

1945 NIL

CUCKFIELD URBAN DISTRICT

1943

26. 6.1943	SPITFIRE	HURSTWOOD PARK	

1944 NIL

1945 NIL

EASTBOURNE COUNTY BOROUGH

1943

11. 2.1943	SPITFIRE	IN THE SEA OFF BEACHY HEAD	
8. 6.1943	DEFIANT	BEACHY HEAD	
20. 6.1943	MUSTANG P51	BEACHY HEAD	
11. 8.1943	SPITFIRE	LANGNEY	
25. 8.1943	MUSTANG P51	IN THE SEA OFF BEACHY HEAD	
9.11.1943	MESSERSCHMITT 410	HAMPDEN PARK	(C45)

1944

2. 2.1944	LIBERATOR B24	RATTON
17. 6.1944	SPITFIRE	IN THE SEA OFF BEACHY HEAD

1945 NIL

EAST GRINSTEAD URBAN DISTRICT

1943 NIL
1944 NIL
1945 NIL

HAILSHAM RURAL DISTRICT

1943

11. 2.1943	SPITFIRE	PEVENSEY	
16. 3.1943	HALIFAX	FRISTON AIRFIELD	
28. 4.1943	TYPHOON	PEVENSEY	
28. 5.1943	SPITFIRE	FRISTON AIRFIELD	
30. 5.1943	SPITFIRE	EAST DEAN	(C36)
4. 6.1943	FOCKE WULF 190	NORMANS BAY	
16. 7.1943	MUSTANG P51	BEACH AT RIVER CUCKMERE	
11. 8.1943	STIRLING	IN THE SEA, NORMANS BAY	
31. 8.1943	FORTRESS B17	POLEGATE	(C41)
6. 9.1943	FORTRESS B17	DEANLAND AIRFIELD	
6. 9.1943	FORTRESS B17	PEVENSEY BAY BEACH	
5.10.1943	HALIFAX	HEATHFIELD	
11.11.1943	MUSTANG P51	HELLINGLY	
31.12.1943	THUNDERBOLT P47	NORMANS BAY	

1944

4. 1.1944	SPITFIRE	HERSTMONCEUX	
14. 1.1944	BOSTON	PEVENSEY	
5. 2.1944	FORTRESS B17	ALFRISTON	(C42)
9. 2.1944	MITCHELL B25	CROWLINK, FRISTON	
28. 2.1944	MARAUDER B26	PEVENSEY MARSH	
4. 3.1944	FORTRESS B17	FRISTON FOREST	
5. 3.1944	MUSTANG P51	RUSHLAKE GREEN	
12. 3.1944	LIBERATOR B24	FRISTON AIRFIELD	
14. 3.1944	DORNIER 217	SEVEN SISTERS, FRISTON	
7. 4.1944	SPITFIRE	GOLDEN CROSS	
7. 4.1944	SPITFIRE	WHITESMITH	
20. 4.1944	BOSTON	FRISTON AIRFIELD	
29. 4.1944	SPITFIRE	GATE FIELD, FRISTON	(C37)
7. 5.1944	SPITFIRE	BIRLING GAP	
17. 5.1944	TEMPEST	DEANLAND	
27. 5.1944	MARAUDER B26	COWBEECH	
28. 5.1944	THUNDERBOLT P47	BROAD OAK, HEATHFIELD	
8. 6.1944	STINSON	POLEGATE	
8. 6.1944	MARAUDER B26	POLEGATE	(C43)
8. 6.1944	MUSTANG P51	LITLINGTON	
8. 6.1944	SPITFIRE	FOLKINGTON	(C38)
13. 6.1944	SPITFIRE	WILLINGDO	(C39)
19. 6.1944	TEMPEST	PEVENSEY	
20. 6.1944	SPITFIRE	NINFIELD	
25. 6.1944	MOSQUITO	PEVENSEY	
28. 6.1944	TEMPEST	JEVINGTON	(C32)
28. 6.1944	MOSQUITO	FRISTON AIRFIELD	
7. 7.1944	TEMPEST	HORSE EYE, PEVENSEY	
9. 7.1944	MARAUDER B26	HAILSHAM	(C44)
10. 7.1944	LANCASTER	IN THE SEA, NORMANS BAY	
12. 7.1944	TEMPEST	SELMESTON	
16. 7.1944	MUSTANG P51	CUCKMERE HAVEN	
18. 7.1944	TEMPEST	BROAD OAK, HEATHFIELD	
20. 7.1944	TEMPEST	LAUGHTON	(C33)
21. 7.1944	LIBERATOR B24	DEANLAND AIRFIELD	
23. 7.1944	TEMPEST	STONE CROSS	(C35)
24. 7.1944	TEMPEST	WILLINGDON	(C34)
26. 7.1944	MOSQUITO	FRISTON AIRFIELD	
10. 9.1944	MOSQUITO	FRISTON AIRFIELD	
30. 9.1944	MITCHELL B25	CHILLEY BRIDGE, PEVENSEY	

1945

6. 2.1945	DAKOTA DC3	WILMINGTON
6. 5.1945	DAKOTA DC3	WILMINGTON

HASTINGS COUNTY BOROUGH

1943

6. 6.1943	SPITFIRE	ST. HELENS ROAD
21.10.1943	TYPHOON	IN THE SEA OFF HASTINGS

1944

19. 6.1944	SPITFIRE	IN THE SEA OFF HASTINGS
7. 7.1944	TEMPEST	IN THE SEA OFF HASTINGS
21. 8.1944	MOSQUITO	IN THE SEA OFF HASTINGS

1945 NIL

HORSHAM RURAL DISTRICT

1943

6.12.1943	SPITFIRE	COLGATE ROAD, HORSHAM

1944

7. 1.1944	MITCHELL B25	PALLINGHURST, RUDGWICK (Collided with aircraft below)
7. 1.1944	MITCHELL B25	PALLINGHURST, RUDGWICK
24. 1.1944	SPITFIRE	STEEPWOOD, BILLINGSHURST
24. 1.1944	HURRICANE	BILLINGSHURST
15. 2.1944	MARAUDER B26	COOLHAM
30. 3.1944	TIGER MOTH	WEST GRINSTEAD
19. 4.1944	MUSTANG	SHIPLEY
19. 4.1944	MESSERSCHMITT 410	NUTHURST
21. 4.1944	MUSTANG P51	COOLHAM AIRSTRIP
19. 5.1944	MUSTANG P51	HONEYWOOD HOUSE, ROWHOOK (Collided with aircraft below)
19. 5.1944	MUSTANG P51	HONEYWOOD HOUSE, ROWHOOK
24. 5.1944	TYPHOON	MAPLEHURST
2. 8.1944	SPITFIRE	DAUX WOOD, BILLINGSHURST
20. 8.1944	FAIRCHILD ARGUS	APPLETREE FARM, IFIELD
6.10.1944	PROCTOR	SOUTHWATER SCHOOL

HORSHAM URBAN DISTRICT

1943

10. 7.1943	TIGER MOTH	WARNHAM
21.11.1943	FOCKE WULF 190	BROADBRIDGE HEATH
6.12.1943	SPITFIRE	ROFFEY CORNER

1944

8. 6.1944	MITCHELL B25	AMIES MILL (Collided with aircraft below)
8. 6.1944	MITCHELL B25	PICTS MILL

1945

17. 2.1945	HALIFAX	MANNINGS HEATH

HOVE MUNICIPAL BOROUGH

1943

2. 4.1943	MOSQUITO	NEAR HOVE CEMETERY	(B54)

1944

16. 3.1944	LIGHTNING P38	IN THE SEA OFF HOVE
23. 5.1944	FORTRESS B17	IN THE SEA OFF HOVE

1945

6. 5.1945	MOSQUITO	DYKE ROAD, HOVE	(B56)

LEWES MUNICIPAL BOROUGH

1943

17. 4.1943	HALIFAX	LANDPORT, LEWES	(C40)

1944 NIL

1945

6. 2.1945	MUSTANG P51	SOUTH MALLING, LEWES

LITTLEHAMPTON URBAN DISTRICT

1943

13. 8.1943	LANCASTER	IN THE SEA OFF LITTLEHAMPTON
21.10.1943	BEAUFIGHTER	PARKSIDE ESTATE, RUSTINGTON

1944

5. 1.1944	SPITFIRE	TOLL BRIDGE, LITTLEHAMPTON
9. 7.1944	THUNDERBOLT P47	IN THE SEA OFF LITTLEHAMPTON

1945

17. 2.1945	MOSQUITO	CHAUCER AVENUE, RUSTINGTON

MIDHURST RURAL DISTRICT

1943

8. 3.1943	DORNIER 217	FERNHURST
19. 3.1943	TIGER MOTH	WARDLEY HANGER
22. 9.1943	TIGER MOTH	NEAR NYEWOOD POST OFFICE
5.11.1943	TIGER MOTH	WOODMANS HATCH GREEN

1944

20. 1.1944 TEMPEST — AMBERSHAM COMMON
25. 1.1944 LIGHTNING P38 — FERNHURST
8. 6.1944 LIGHTNING P38 — BEPTON
30. 6.1944 LANCASTER — PITSHAM COMMON
4. 7.1944 LIGHTNING P38 — GRAFFHAM

1945

9. 2.1945 AUSTER — STEDHAM
12. 4.1945 TIGER MOTH — ELSTED
2. 5.1945 SPITFIRE — FERNHURST

NEWHAVEN URBAN DISTRICT

1943

20. 8.1943 WELLINGTON — IN THE SEA OFF NEWHAVEN

1944

12. 7.1944 SPITFIRE — THE DROVE, NEWHAVEN (C48)

1945 NIL

PETWORTH RURAL DISTRICT

1943

13. 8.1943 LANCASTER — PLAISTOW
19. 8.1943 FULMAR — FISHER STREET FARM, NORTH CHAPEL

1944

3. 4.1944 SPITFIRE — SUTTON
8. 4.1944 MILES MAGISTER — SHILLINGLEE
25. 6.1944 MUSTANG P51 — KEY FOX FARM, PETWORTH

1945 NIL

PORTSLADE URBAN DISTRICT

1943 NIL

1944

6. 6.1944 HAVOC — PORTSLADE (B62)

1945 NIL

RYE MUNICIPAL BOROUGH

1943 NIL
1944 NIL
1945 NIL

SEAFORD URBAN DISTRICT

1943

10. 7.1943 HALIFAX — FORESHORE SEAFORD (C50)
30. 7.1943 AUSTER — BISHOPSTONE
25. 8.1943 MUSTANG P51 — IN THE SEA OFF DANE ROAD

1944

25. 2.1944 TYPHOON — SEAFORD HEAD
18. 5.1944 SPITFIRE — SEAFORD BAY
28. 8.1944 LIGHTNING P38 — BLATCHINGTON
26.10.1944 AUSTER — SEAFORD CHESTERTON SCHOOL

1945 NIL

SHOREHAM-BY-SEA URBAN DISTRICT

1943

20. 1.1943 BEAUFIGHTER — IN THE SEA OFF SHOREHAM
12. 4.1943 STIRLING — IN THE SEA OFF SHOREHAM
14. 7.1943 THUNDERBOLT P47 — IN THE SEA OFF SHOREHAM
12. 8.1943 WELLINGTON — IN THE SEA OFF SHOREHAM

1944 NIL

1945

21. 4.1945 SPITFIRE — IN THE SEA OFF SHOREHAM HARBOUR

SOUTHWICK URBAN DISTRICT

1943 NIL
1944 NIL
1945 NIL

UCKFIELD RURAL DISTRICT

1943

13. 2.1943 TYPHOON — DANE HILL
30. 5.1943 JUNKERS 88 — BARCOMBE
9. 6.1943 SPITFIRE — ROTHERFIELD
6. 9.1943 FORTRESS B17 — ASHDOWN FOREST
10. 9.1943 PROCTOR — NUTLEY
5.10.1943 HALIFAX — MAYFIELD
17.10.1943 TYPHOON — ASHDOWN FOREST
15.12.1943 SPITFIRE — FOREST ROW

1944

26. 1.1944 MARAUDER B26 — CROWBOROUGH
23. 2.1944 JUNKERS 188 — FRAMFIELD
23. 2.1944 MESSERSCHMITT 410 — HALLAND
24. 2.1944 JUNKERS 188 — WITHYHAM
2. 3.1944 HEINKEL 177 — HAMMERWOOD
7. 4.1944 TYPHOON — PILTDOWN
6. 5.1944 TYPHOON — PILTDOWN
16. 5.1944 SPITFIRE — NUTLEY
9. 6.1944 TYPHOON — MAYFIELD
22. 6.1944 LANCASTER — ROTHERFIELD
12. 7.1944 MARAUDER B26 — FOREST ROW
26. 7.1944 SPITFIRE — RIDGEWOOD

1945

9. 2.1945 TIGER MOTH — HORSEGROVE FARM, ROTHERFIELD
21. 3.1945 SPITFIRE — COLEMANS HATCH

WORTHING MUNICIPAL BOROUGH

1943

19. 3.1943 HAMPDEN — IN THE SEA OFF WORTHING
27. 3.1943 JUNKERS 88 — IN THE SEA OFF HEENE ROAD
1. 7.1943 TIGER MOTH — SOMPTING (B60)
26. 8.1943 MARAUDER B26 — KINGSTON-ON-SEA
24.10.1943 AUTOGIRO — IN THE SEA OFF WORTHING

1944

22. 1.1944 JUNKERS 88 — IN THE SEA OFF WORTHING
17.12.1944 LANCASTER — IN THE SEA OFF WORTHING (B58)

1945 NIL

WORTHING RURAL DISTRICT

1943

17. 6.1943 TYPHOON — FINDON (B28)
21.11.1943 MOSQUITO — LYMINSTER
30.11.1943 WHITLEY — LANCING (B57)

1944

31. 1.1944 MOSQUITO — POLING
6. 3.1944 MOSQUITO — SEA LANE, FERRING
7. 5.1944 SPITFIRE — FINDON VALLEY (B61)
1. 8.1944 MUSTANG — BURPHAM
3. 8.1944 SPITFIRE — COOMBES

1945

25. 4.1945 ALBACORE — THE DOWNS, WORTHING (B59)

THE WAR IN SUSSEX A BRIEF STATISTICAL SUMMARY

High explosive Bombs	11,486
Small Incendiary Bombs	89,765
Other Incendiary Bombs	341
Parachute Mines + Bombs	77
Anti-Personnel Bombs	1,405
Flying Bombs (V1s)	907
Rockets (V2s)	4
Persons Killed	1,015
Persons Injured	3,895
Enemy Aircraft Down *	152
Enemy Aircrew Killed	220
Enemy Aircrew POW	152
Allied Aircraft Down *	715
Allied Aircrew Killed	533
Allied Aircrew Safe	1,055

N.B.* These figures do not include aircraft in the sea or on designated airfields.

All of the above information has been extracted from official wartime records. The authors cannot vouch for the 100% accuracy of these figures.

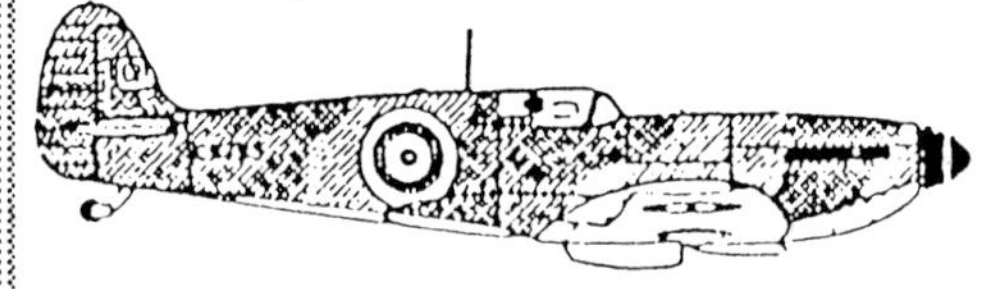